# ROME
## Like a Local

BY THE PEOPLE WHO CALL IT HOME

# ROME

## Like a Local

BY THE PEOPLE WHO CALL IT HOME

# Contents

## NIGHTLIFE



## OUTDOORS



## meet the locals

### LIZA KARSEMEIJER

*Dutch-born freelance journalist Liza moved to Rome in 2018 for "a year or two", but ended up staying for five, drawn to its unpretentious character.*

### EMMA LAW

*Emma ignored the naysayers and moved to Rome in 2014. Now a marketing consultant, you'll find her swirling spaghetti at trattorias and making a list of favourite* gelaterie.

### FEDERICA RUSTICO

*Blogger Federica has lived all over, but Rome is her favourite place. She can be found enjoying* aperitivi *at trendy bars and exploring the city.*

### ANDREA STRAFILE

*Born in Milan, Andrea is a freelance writer and editor-in-chief at* Munchies Italia. *He loves the Porta Portese flea market and messily eating a red Roman pizza.*

# Rome

## WELCOME TO THE CITY

Undeniably, Rome is one of the world's great cities. Its iconic ancient ruins have long graced history books, its vibrant cobbled streets have been immortalized in fashion magazines and its effortless charm (or *sprezzatura*, as it's known here) has imbued many an iconic film. This is the Eternal City, after all – a place that will never go out of style.

Timeless, elegant and bursting with history, it's a city that everyone thinks they know. But Rome is so much more than the sum of its ancient parts. Above all, it's a place where people *live*, and, make no mistake, life is lived nonchalantly around those famous monuments. Workers deftly park their bright Vespas outside art-filled galleries, morning shoppers browse bustling markets set up beside Renaissance fountains and friends linger over drinks in centuries-old piazzas. And while history and tradition will always be upheld, just as much space is made for the modern. Street artists decorate the walls of former working-class areas, innovative chefs give generations-old recipes a creative spin and rock bands take to the stage in gritty underground music venues, keeping the capital as fresh as they come. The people of Rome really are at the heart of the city – just as much as the Colosseum and the Trevi Fountain – and so who better to ask to create this travel guide?

No doubt, you'll come to Rome to visit the Vatican or climb up the Spanish Steps (and you should do both), but we say make time for the simple things, too. Enjoy an *aperitivo* while people-watching on a little street near an imposing palazzo, or perhaps a steaming slice of pizza before a game at the Foro Italico. So, come on, listen to the locals, do away with that to-do list and indulge in *la dolce vita*. It's hard not to when in Rome, after all.

## Liked by the locals

**"The first time I visited Rome as a kid, I knew I was going to live here. Now, there is nothing that warms my soul more than seeing the Colosseum while I drive past, or listening to older Romans arguing. Every time I come back from a trip, I realize that I have made the best choice of my life."**

ANDREA STRAFILE,
WRITER AND EDITOR

*From city-wide celebrations in the spring to glitzy festivals and art show openings come autumn, each season offers another great way to enjoy Rome.*

# Rome THROUGH THE YEAR

## SPRING

### PASQUETTA

While Easter celebrations are taken seriously in Rome, it's Pasquetta (Easter Monday) that young Romans treasure the most, spending it outdoors with friends, barbecues, wine and music.

### NATALE DI ROMA

Every year, the Eternal City celebrates its founding on 21 April with parades, historical re-enactments, free museum days and festivities.

### LABOUR DAY

If Romans aren't enjoying a seaside lunch on Labour Day (1 May), they'll be at the free concert at Piazza San Giovanni, with its roster of Italian artists.

## SUMMER

### ALFRESCO HANGOUTS

As the hot summer sun sets, Romans head outdoors: piazzas bustle, outdoor film screenings start, riverside festivals like Lungo il Tevere begin and rooftop bars become the place to be.

### BEACH TIME

All of Rome moves to the beach for sunny *aperitivi* in August. You'll struggle to find anywhere open in town during the weeks around the Italian public holiday of Ferragosto (15 August).

### SAGRE

Summertime is synonymous with *sagre*, or small-town festivals centred around a characteristic food or drink of the area.

The Castelli Romani area hosts the *Infiorata di Genzano* (flower festival) in June, while Ariccia marks *Sagra della Porchetta* (pork roast) in September.

## AUTUMN

### OTTOBRATE ROMANE

Locals love the sunny *ottobrate romane* (Roman October), which feels more like a second summer than the start of autumn. They take advantage of the good weather to go on day trips and take part in the olive harvest.

### ROME FILM FESTIVAL

Rome was nicknamed "Hollywood on the Tiber" in the 1950s, and the city's annual October film festival lives up to this legacy. It's when A-listers flock to the Auditorium Parco della Musica for international movie premieres.

### EXHIBITIONS TIME

Autumn is prime time for art shows in Rome. Some of the most popular galleries and museums – like Chiostro del Bramante, Palazzo Bonaparte and the MAXXI – open their biggest and most hotly anticipated exhibitions as the weather starts to turn cooler.

### ROMA JAZZ FESTIVAL

November is all about jazz in Rome. While each edition of the Roma Jazz Festival celebrates a different sub-genre, the one thing that never changes is the quality, with prominent musicians performing across different venues.

## WINTER

### HOLIDAY CHEER

Christmas in Rome is full of traditions, from the lighting of trees and opening of sparkling Christmas markets in early December, to the arrival of La Befana, an older lady who delivers gifts to children on 6 January.

### HIT THE SLOPES

Romans are always up for some winter fun, whether it's a full week of skiing or a day trip to the nearby resorts of Ovindoli, Roccaraso or Campo Felice. Either way, these trips usually end with some hearty mountain food.

### WINTER SALES

Shopaholics eagerly await January, when winter sales hit, offering a chance to revamp their wardrobes or score stylish, high-end pieces at a bargain.

*There's an art to being a Roman, from the dos and don'ts of ordering a coffee to navigating the city's busy streets. Here's a breakdown of all you need to know.*

# Rome

## KNOW-HOW

For a directory of health and safety resources, safe spaces and accessibility information, turn to page 186. For everything else, read on.

### EAT

You don't need us to tell you that food is sacred in Rome. Breakfast is a light but indulgent affair, consisting of a coffee and pastry, while lunch (anytime between noon and 3pm) is often a plate of pasta or pizza by the slice. Dinner is the main meal of the day, when Romans sit down with their loved ones from 8pm onwards. A word to the wise: always book ahead. Locals spend hours savouring dinner so tables can be scarce.

### DRINK

Like all Italians, Romans are powered by coffee. Espressos are usually enjoyed quickly at the counter, cappuccinos equally so (though some may sit for the latter). Oh, and a cappuccino is *never* ordered after 12pm, unless you want to attract some eye rolls. Likewise traditional coffee shops don't approve of laptops – you're here to enjoy your coffee and the ambience, after all.

Lunch is accompanied by a glass of wine or beer, and the end of the day toasted with an *aperitivo*. This Italian happy hour takes place from 6pm.

### SHOP

All the usual suspects line Rome's streets but locals love to shop at one-off stores and markets (where haggling is acceptable). Shops are generally open from 10am to 7.30pm, though small businesses often close for lunch anytime between 1 and 3pm. These shops are usually closed on Sundays, too, while chain stores and malls remain open.

## ARTS & CULTURE

Rome is an open-air museum so there's loads to see for free. That said, most museums and big sights charge €12–20 for admission (unless it's the first Sunday of the month, when they're free) and queues can be long, so buying tickets online is worth it. Visiting lots of galleries and museums? Consider the Roma Pass, which grants free or reduced entry to many. If you're stepping inside one of Rome's 900 churches, don't forget to cover your knees and shoulders. *www.romapass.it*

## NIGHTLIFE

Rome's nightlife is very laid-back (you don't need to dress up) and revolves around the city's bars. The evening kicks off with an *aperitivo* before dinner and, for those wanting the night to continue, post-dinner drinks. On those nights when locals want to go hard, they move on to the city's clubs, which generally get going around midnight. Our advice? Pace yourself and savour that *aperitivo* (one drink, one snack). It's not a good look to get drunk in Rome.

## OUTDOORS

For locals, the outdoors is an extension of the home; parks are treated as back gardens, piazzas as living rooms. And a day isn't complete without an afternoon *passeggiata* (stroll). Be mindful that eating on Rome's monuments and fountains can be frowned upon. This regulation isn't universally enforced but we advise against it all the same.

## Keep in mind

**Here are some other tips and tidbits that will help you fit in like a local.**

» **Carry cash** Most places accept contactless payments over €5, but many markets are cash-only.

» **Tipping** Tips aren't required but they are appreciated. Leave a few coins at a café or 5–10 percent of the total bill at restaurants.

» **Smoking** A lot of Italians smoke, but lighting up indoors is banned, so only do so when you're on a café terrace or in a piazza.

» **Stay hydrated** There are plenty of water fountains so bring a reusable bottle. If you ask nicely, café staff will refill your bottle too.

## GETTING AROUND

Rome's vast sprawl comprises 22 *rioni* (districts) that spiral out from the ancient heart of the city, where the Roman Forum and Colosseum stand proud. Cutting the city almost perfectly in half is the Tiber, which runs north to south and separates the likes of Prati, Trastevere and Monteverde from the aforementioned stalwarts. For locals, whichever side of the river they live, there's a cultural distinction between a historically working-class southern Rome and well-off northern Rome.

We'll be honest: navigating Rome can be tricky. The city is, in large part, a tangle of ancient roads, and street names and building numbers can be hard to spot. To make life easier, we've provided what3words addresses for each sight in this book, so you can pinpoint exactly where you're heading.

### On foot

It might be a metropolis but Rome is best explored on foot, especially the winding streets of the compact historic centre, which wasn't built with cars in mind. Romans aren't often in a hurry but they can get a bit short-tempered when stuck behind wide-eyed tourists. So, if you need to check a what3words location or take a photo, step aside to let them pass. Finally, while the temptation to put on your new leather sandals or brogues may be hard to resist, wear comfy shoes – this city has seven hills to traverse, remember.

### On wheels

Cycling is not for the faint of heart in a city of horn-happy drivers and roaring Vespas. If you're willing to brave it, cycle in single file as much as possible, use hand signals when turning, ensure you have appropriate bike lights and always wear a helmet (it's the law). We definitely recommend renting two wheels for outside of the city centre, especially along the ancient Appian Way *(p185)* and along the banks of the Tiber, where things are much more relaxed.

Lime, Tier and Dott rental bikes have a monopoly in Rome, with electric, pedal-assist bikes giving riders an extra boost. Simply find a bike (they're dotted across the city), scan its QR code to unlock it and fully retract the cable lock in order to free up the wheels. There's no need to return it to the same spot; just be sure to leave it somewhere sensible and remember to lock it again once you've finished your journey.

*www.li.me*
*www.ridedott.com*
*www.tier.app*

## By public transport

Rome's public transport system, which is run by the ATAC, mainly comprises tramway, trolleybus, bus and metro lines. If we're honest, the network isn't always the most efficient way of getting around; it can be unreliable and over-crowded. Tickets across all modes of transport cost €1.50 and can be purchased at any *tabacchi* (look out for the blue T), newsstand or metro station. Be sure to scan your ticket upon entry or else you risk being fined. The train network, meanwhile, is excellent and runs like clockwork, with Rome well connected to other cities (like Florence and Naples) and towns in Lazio.

## By car and taxi

Driving in Rome isn't easy and finding a parking spot is a nightmare, not least because most Romans drive or ride Vespas because they don't trust the metro to get then from A to B. If you're looking to join them, car-sharing services like Share Now are a good option. As for taxis, the city has a large fleet of licensed cabs, which can either be hailed on the street or called in advance. Alternatively, visit the Free Now website or download the app to book a ride.

*www.free-now.com*
*www.share-now.com*

# Download these

**We recommend you download these apps to help you get about the city.**

### WHAT3WORDS

**Your geocoding friend**

A what3words address is a simple way to communicate any precise location on earth, using just three words. ///survive.bunks.dignity, for example, is the code for the central fountain in Piazza Navona. Simply download the free what3words app, type a what3words address into the search bar, and you'll know exactly where to go.

### CITYMAPPER

**Your journey planner**

Transportation apps for Rome are hit and miss (largely because the network itself isn't the best) so locals prefer to use trusty old Citymapper. The route planner offers live info on the best routes, using buses, bikes, taxis and more. There's real-time info on departures and delays, too.

***Rome is a vast mosaic of neighbourhoods, and locals are fiercely loyal of the patch they hail from. Here we take a look at some of our favourites.***

# Rome NEIGHBOURHOODS

## Campo de' Fiori

Known to locals simply as "Campo", this square buzzes during the day thanks to its top-notch fruit and veg market. As market traders pack away their wares, locals return for an *aperitivo* in the area's cosy bars. *{map 1}*

## Campo Marzio

When it comes to shopping for their uber-chic wardrobes, locals head straight to Campo Marzio. You'll find the big chains here but tucked behind these designer giants are small, timeless boutiques. *{map 4}*

## Centocelle

Don't be fooled by this area's suburban 1960s architecture. Centocelle has seen a foodie revolution in recent years, with a trendy restaurant on every street corner. *{map 6}*

## Esquilino

Nowhere embodies modern Rome better than Esquilino. Chinese and Ethiopian families call this place home, paving the way for a fab food scene. *{map 4}*

## Flaminio

Modern architecture, vintage markets and stylish bars: Flaminio oozes elegance. No wonder locals aspire to live here. *{map 5}*

## Garbatella

Built during Mussolini's rule, Garbatella was intended for factory workers. These days, a varied bunch live here, and community is king; locals wave at one another across their apartment block courtyards and chat to the table next to them in their favourite trattoria. *{map 3}*

## Jewish Quarter

In the 1500s, the Jewish community was forced to live in this walled quarter, with their rights hugely restricted. Fast-forward to today and the quarter is a hub of Jewish culture and tradition. Its Roman-Jewish cuisine will change your life (remember: places close for Shabbat). *{map 1}*

## Monteverde

Across the Tiber from the tourist sights, Monteverde makes for a lovely retreat.

Tree-lined streets, leafy parks, relaxed pizzerias: this is the place to enjoy a slower pace of life. *{map 3}*

## Monti

Forget what you've heard about Trastevere – Monti is where it's at. Small businesses run by jovial baristas, master gelato makers and antique experts make this pretty neighbourhood *the* place to put down roots. Or at least stay for a weekend. *{map 4}*

## Ostiense

Colourful murals, street food joints and LGBTQ+-friendly hangouts tempt young professionals to while away their weekends exploring gritty Ostiense. *{map 3}*

## Parioli

Large avenues dotted with elegant villas and bougie bars characterize this posh patch. It's an after-hours playground for Rome's rich and famous. *{map 5}*

## Piazza Navona

Slap-bang in the middle of Rome, this oval-shaped piazza is home to grand Baroque fountains and seriously touristy pavement cafés. Romans know better; they prefer to linger over their wine in one of the traditional bars tucked down the streets bounding the piazza. *{map 1}*

## Pigneto

Despite looming gentrification, cool kid on the block Pigneto remains rough around the edges. Street art and vegan cafés make this edgy area a hipster's paradise. *{map 6}*

## Prati

This white-collar neighbourhood throngs with office workers going about their business during the week. But, come the weekend, locals pour in to sip coffees and enjoy an afternoon stroll with stellar views of St Peter's Basilica. *{map 5}*

## San Lorenzo

Once a working-class community, San Lorenzo was heavily bombed during World War II. But this is not a neighbourhood to be beaten down. The area's resilience is reflected in its creativity. Pop by a bookshop event or burlesque bar to see it for yourself. *{map 6}*

## Testaccio

An old slaughterhouse stands stalwart in Testaccio, a reminder of the neighbourhood's meatpacking past. Descendants of abattoir workers shop for supplies in their tantalizing local food market. They're not alone: Romans will journey across the city for a first-rate lunch here. *{map 3}*

## Trastevere

Yes, tourists have clocked onto Trastevere's charming cobbled streets and old-school trattorias but this enclave hasn't lost its charm. Retired Romans spend their afternoons playing cards in their favourite corners of the area, lines of laundry flapping overhead. *{map 2}*

## Trevi

While tourists come here to throw a coin in the world's most famous fountain, locals head straight to the area's lovely cafés for a caffeine hit. *{map 4}*

# Rome

## ON THE MAP

*Whether you're looking for your new favourite spot or want to check out what each part of Rome has to offer, our maps – along with handy map references throughout the book – have you covered.*

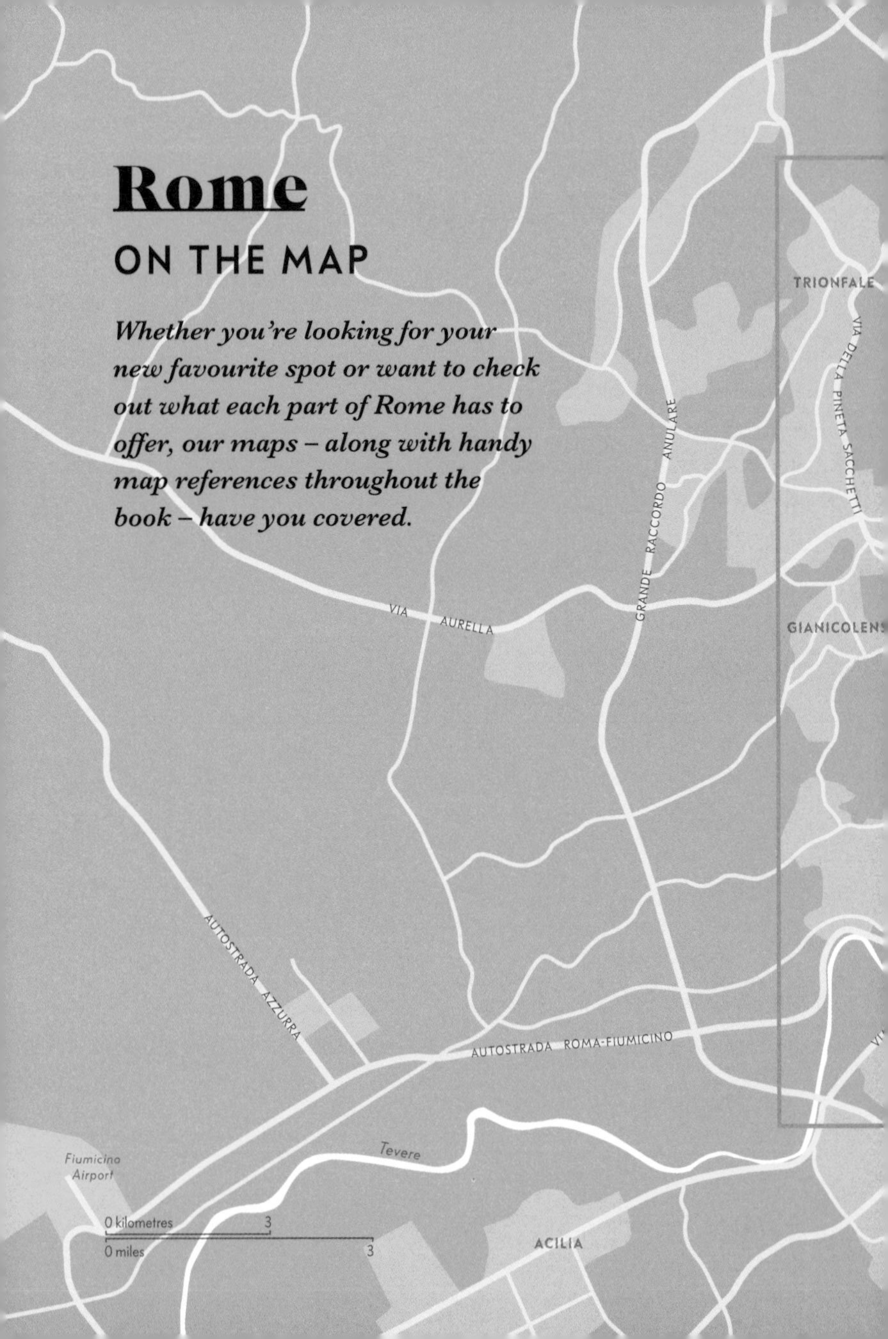

VIA CASSIA
Tevere
VIA SALARIA
VIGNA CLARA
TUFELLO
GRANDE RACCORDO ANULARE
6
5
VIA NOMENTANA
FLAMINIO
TRIESTE
PIETRALATA
PRATI
4
LA RUSTICA
STRADA DEI PARCHI
1
VIA PRENESTINA
PIGNETO
2
CENTOCELLE
VIA CASILINA
OSTIENSE
QUADRARO
3
VIA TUSCOLANA
CINECITTÀ
PORTUENSE
VIA APPIA NUOVA
SAN PAOLO
ROMANINA
Tevere
VIA DEL MARE
CAPANNELLE
EUR
VIA LAURENTINA
VIA PONTINA
VIA ARDEATINA
VIA APPIA ANTICA
CECCHIGNOLA
CIAMPINO
GRANDE RACCORDO ANULARE

Castel Sant'Angelo
PIAZZA DEI TRIBUNALI
Tevere
VIA DI CLEMENTINO
LUNGOTEVERE CASTELLO
Ponte Umberto I
VIA MONTE BRIANZO
Ponte Sant' Angelo
La Cravatta su Misura S
Retrobottega E
Booktique S
LUNGOTEVERE TOR DI NONA
V. ZANARDELLI
Palazzo Altemps A
PIAZZA DI S. SALVATORE IN LAURO
Co.Ro. Jewels S
Club Derrière N
Essenzialmente Laura S
VIA DEI CORONARI
Andreano S
V. DEL BANCO S. SPIRITO
CORSO VITTORIO EMANUELE II
PONTE
Mater Terrae E
Chiostro del Bramante A
VIA DELLA SCROFA
VIA DELLA
VIA GIULIA
VIA DEL GOVERNO VECCHIO
Bar del Fico D
Fountain of Four Rivers A
CORSO DEL RINASCIMENTO
PIAZZA NAVONA
Piazza Navona O
PIAZZA DI SANT'EUSTACHIO
PARIONE
The Jerry Thomas Project N
PIAZZA D. CHIESA NUOVA
Omero e Cecilia S
Enoteca Il Piccolo D
Otherwise S
Caffè Sant'Eustachio D
LT. D. SANGALLO
Il Goccetto D
Faraoni S
Frissón N
Pipero E
Wisdomless Club N
Altroquando S
La Montecarlo E
Italo dal 1968 S
VIA DEL PELLEGRINO
CORSO VITTORIO EMANUELE II
Cash Diner Club N
VIA DI TORRE ARGENTINA
VIA DI MONSERRATO
Argot N
PIAZZA D. CANCELLERIA
Ponte G. Mazzini
Forno Campo de' Fiori E
Bar Farnese D
LUNGOTEVERE DEI TEBALDI
Mercato di Campo de' Fiori S
Piazza Campo de' Fiori O
Caffè Perù D
CAMPO DE' FIORI
PIAZZA FARNESE
Il Vinaietto D
Tevere
VIA GIULIA
Dar Filettaro E
LARGO ARENU
LUNGOTEVERE DELLA FARNESINA
VIA DELLA LUNGARA
Salumeria Roscioli E
PIAZZA B. CAIROLI
Gran Caffè Rione VIII D
Galleria Spada A
Galleria Lorcan O'Neill A
Open Baladin D
Beppe e i suoi Formaggi N
VIA DEI RIARI
ANGELO
Hey Guey rooftop at Chapter Roma N
Al Pompiere E
Ponte Sisto
Orto Botanico
Bar del Cappuccino E
LUNGOT. DEI VALLATI
PIAZZA TRILUSSA
LUNGOT. R. SANZIO
VIA DELLA SCALA
Ponte Garibaldi
0 metres 200
0 yards 200
TRASTEVERE

## E EAT

Al Pompiere *(p41)*
Bar del Cappuccino *(p35)*
Dar Filettaro *(p34)*
Forno Boccione *(p37)*
Forno Campo de' Fiori *(p33)*
La Montecarlo *(p46)*
Mater Terrae *(p51)*
Pipero *(p55)*
Retrobottega *(p54)*
Salumeria Roscioli *(p52)*

## D DRINK

Bar Farnese *(p64)*
Bar del Fico *(p66)*
Caffè Perù *(p67)*
Caffè Sant'Eustachio *(p62)*
Enoteca Il Piccolo *(p73)*
Gran Caffè Rione VIII *(p61)*
Il Goccetto *(p73)*
Il Vinaietto *(p75)*
Open Baladin *(p79)*
Tazza d'Oro *(p61)*

## S SHOP

Altroquando *(p100)*
Andreano *(p95)*
Booktique *(p101)*
Co.Ro. Jewels *(p92)*
Essenzialmente Laura *(p95)*
Faraoni *(p94)*
Gammarelli Sartoria *(p88)*
Italo dal 1968 *(p97)*
La Cravatta su Misura *(p88)*
Mercato di Campo de' Fiori *(p85)*
Omero e Cecilia *(p98)*
Otherwise *(p100)*

## A ARTS & CULTURE

Chiostro del Bramante *(p129)*
Fontana delle Tartarughe *(p133)*
Fountain of Four Rivers *(p135)*
Galleria Lorcan O'Neill *(p130)*
Galleria Spada *(p127)*
The Jewish Museum *(p116)*
Palazzo Altemps *(p115)*
Pantheon *(p114)*

## N NIGHTLIFE

Argot *(p150)*
Beppe e i suoi Formaggi *(p143)*
Cash Diner Club *(p155)*
Club Derrière *(p149)*
Frissón *(p153)*
Hey Guey rooftop at Chapter Roma *(p140)*
The Jerry Thomas Project *(p148)*
Salotto 42 *(p140)*
Wisdomless Club *(p151)*

## O OUTDOORS

Lungotevere *(p167)*
Piazza Campo de' Fiori *(p174)*
Piazza Navona *(p174)*
Piazza della Rotonda *(p175)*

PARIONE
CORSO VITTORIO
Ponte G. Mazzini
VIA DI MONSERRATO
VIA GIULIA
CAMPO DE' FIORI
PIAZZA FARNESE
V. D. GIUBBONARI
Tevere
Vo.Re.Co.
LUNGOTEVERE DELLA FARNESINA
VIA DELLA LUNGARA
Orto Botanico di Roma
Janiculum Hill
Ma Che Siete Venuti A Fà
Ponte Sisto
PIAZZALE GIUSEPPE GARIBALDI
Pizzeria l'Elementare
Trapizzino
Freni e Frizioni
Enoteca l'Antidoto
Ponte Garibaldi
Anna Retico Design
Almost Corner Shop
Trattoria Da Augusto
Alla Fonte d'Oro
VIA GARIBALDI
Libreria Trastevere
VIA D. LUNGARETTA
Piazza di Santa Maria
Tempietto del Bramante
Bar San Calisto
TRASTEVERE
VIALE DI TRASTEVERE
PIAZZALE AURELIO
Bar Gianicolo
Otaleg
Ai Marmi
VIA L. MANARA
Antica Caciara
Drogheria Innocenzi
PIAZZA MASTAI
Alcazar Live
Zia Restaurant
PIAZZA DI. S. COSIMATO
Supplì
VIA G. MAMELI
VIA CALANDRELLI
VIA GIACINTO CARINI
Villa Sciarra
Porta Portese
0 metres 250
0 yards 250

## EAT

Ai Marmi *(p46)*
Otaleg *(p38)*
Supplì *(p34)*
Trapizzino *(p35)*
Trattoria Da Augusto *(p43)*
Zia Restaurant *(p53)*

## DRINK

Alla Fonte d'Oro *(p68)*
Bar Gianicolo *(p65)*
Bar San Calisto *(p66)*
Enoteca l'Antidoto *(p72)*
Ma Che Siete Venuti A Fà *(p77)*
Pizzeria l'Elementare *(p79)*
Sora Mirella *(p71)*

## SHOP

Almost Corner Shop *(p102)*
Anna Retico Design *(p93)*
Antica Caciara *(p107)*
Biscottificio Innocenti *(p105)*
Drogheria Innocenzi *(p106)*
Libreria Trastevere *(p103)*
Open Door Bookshop *(p102)*
Porta Portese *(p87)*
Vo.Re.Co. *(p96)*

## ARTS & CULTURE

Ponte Sisto *(p132)*
Tempietto del Bramante *(p134)*

## NIGHTLIFE

Alcazar Live *(p147)*
Freni e Frizioni *(p142)*

## OUTDOORS

Janiculum Hill *(p165)*
Orto Botanico di Roma *(p170)*
Piazza di Santa Maria *(p175)*

PALATINE
Palatine Hill
Rhinoceros
Circoletto
Bocca della Verità
Garum Museo della Cucina
PIAZZA S. MARIA IN TRASTEVERE
TRASTEVERE
VIA G. GARIBALDI
PIAZZA MASTAI
Parco di Savello
VIA DEL CIRCO MASSIMO
LUNGOTEVERE AVENTINO
Tronchi Morti by Andrea Gandini
PORTA CAPENA
Tevere
Aventine Hill
VIALE DI TRASTEVERE
Villa Sciarra
Ponte Sublicio
RIPA
VIALE AVENTINO
VIA PORTUENSE
VIA A. G. BARRILI
VIA A. POERIO
Giolitti
VIA MARMORATA
PIAZZA ALBINA
Torcè
Antonio Aglietti Shoemaker
PIAZZA ALBANIA
Seu Illuminati
Treefolk's Public House
Piazza Testaccio
Chiosco
Salumeria Volpetti
Tram Depot
PIAZZA G. BERNINI
Mordi e Vai
Jumping Wolf by Roa
Mercato di Testaccio
MONTEVERDE
TESTACCIO
Pyramid of Caius Cestius
PIAZZALE OSTIENSE
Caffè Tevere
Checchino dal 1887
Ponte Testaccio
VIALE MARCO POLO
PIAZZA V. BOTTEGO
La Tavernaccia da Bruno
Marigold
Legs
Murals by Blu
Città Ecosolidale
Städlin
Hunting Pollution by Iena Cruz
VIA A. PACINOTTI
Ponte dell' Industria
VIA OSTIENSE
Romeow Cat Bistrot
OSTIENSE
VIA QUIRINO MAJORANA
VIALE GUGLIELMO MARCONI
CIRCONVALLAZIONE OSTIENSE
Centrale Montemartini
Circolo degli Illuminati
PIAZZA B. ROMANO
GARBATELLA
0 metres 500
0 yards 500
Tevere
Ponte G. Marconi
Parco Schuster
LARGO D. SETTE CHIESE

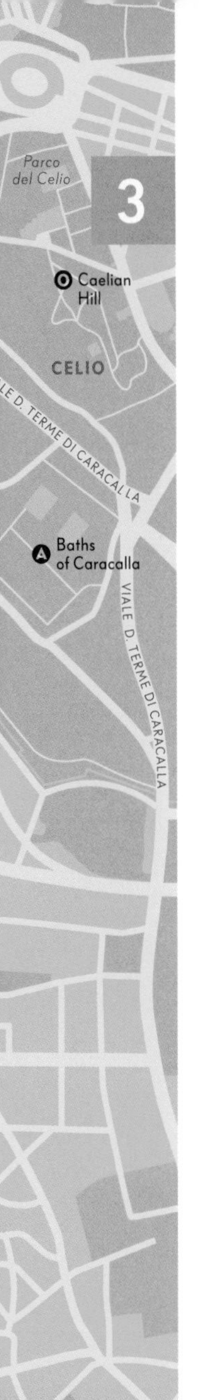




## EAT

Checchino dal 1887 *(p41)*
Giolitti *(p38)*
La Tavernaccia da Bruno *(p43)*
Legs *(p32)*
Marigold *(p48)*
Mordi e Vai *(p33)*
Romeow Cat Bistrot *(p51)*
Seu Illuminati *(p45)*
Torcè *(p36)*

## DRINK

Caffè Tevere *(p67)*
Chiosco *(p68)*
Circoletto *(p75)*
Tram Depot *(p60)*
Treefolk's Public House *(p76)*

## SHOP

Antonio Aglietti Shoemaker *(p90)*
Città Ecosolidale *(p87)*
Salumeria Volpetti *(p104)*
Mercato di Testaccio *(p84)*

## ARTS & CULTURE

Baths of Caracalla *(p134)*
Bocca della Verità *(p134)*
Centrale Montemartini *(p124)*
Garum Museo della Cucina *(p127)*
Hunting Pollution by Iena Cruz *(p123)*
Jumping Wolf by Roa *(p121)*
Murals by Blu *(p123)*
Pyramid of Caius Cestius *(p115)*
Rhinoceros *(p130)*
Tronchi Morti by Andrea Gandini *(p123)*

## NIGHTLIFE

Circolo degli Illuminati *(p156)*
Städlin *(p154)*

## OUTDOORS

Aventine Hill *(p176)*
Caelian Hill *(p178)*
Palatine Hill *(p176)*
Piazza Testaccio *(p174)*

Villa Borghese
Galoppatoio
Viale del Muro Torto
Corso d'Italia
Piazza Fiume
Faro
Via Piave
Porta Pia
Via Vittorio Veneto
Via F. Crispi
Campo Marzio
Sallustiano
Pastificio Guerra
Piazza di Spagna
Antico Caffè Greco
Keats-Shelley Memorial House
Via dei Condotti
Museum and Crypt of the Capuchin Friars
Via L. Bissolati
Via Venti Settembre
Via Cernaia
Trimani Enoteca
Castro Pretorio
Rifugio Romano
Piazza San Bernardo
Baths of Diocletian
Piazza D. Indipendenza
Tartufi dal Bosco
Galleria d'Arte Moderna
Piazza Barberini
Piazza D. Repubblica
Viale E. de Nicola
Piazza di S. Silvestro
Largo D. Tritone
Via del Tritone
Viminal Hill
Piazza D. Cinquecento
Largo Chigi
Trevi
Giardini del Quirinale
Stazione Centrale Roma Termini
Piazza di Trevi
Rome Opera House
Via del Quirinale
Via Giovanni Giolitti
Via del Corso
Pigna
Quirinal Hill
Via della Pilotta
Via Cavour
Via Nazionale
Piazza dell' Esquilino
Piazza M. Fanti
Monti
Galleria Doria Pamphilj
Atelier Marloes Mandaat
Blackmarket Hall
Aromaticus
Grezzo Raw Chocolate
Domus Romane
Via Carlo Alberto
Via Panisperna
Piazza Venezia
Hang Roma
Pifebo
Trajan's Markets
Piazza S. Martino ai Monti
La Bottega del Caffè
Pasticceria Regoli
Victor Emmanuel II Monument
Piazza della Madonna dei Monti
Humana Vintage
King Size
Frab's at Contemporary Cluster
Panella
Via dei Fori Imperiali
Capitoline Hill
Capitoline Museums
Parco di Traiano
Esquiline Hill
Via Merulana
Via D. Teatro di Marcello
Forum
Domus Aurea
Campitelli
Colosseum
The Court
Via Labicana
The Race Club
The Barber Shop
Tevere
Via San Giovanni in Laterano
Via di San Gregorio
Via Claudia
Palatine
Parco del Celio
0 metres
500
0 yards
500

## E EAT

Aromaticus *(p49)*

Gelateria Fassi *(p36)*

Grezzo Raw Chocolate *(p38)*

Pasticceria Regoli *(p37)*

Pastificio Guerra *(p34)*

Rifugio Romano *(p48)*

## D DRINK

Antico Caffè Greco *(p63)*

Faro *(p60)*

La Bottega del Caffè *(p64)*

## S SHOP

Atelier Marloes Mandaat *(p94)*

Frab's at Contemporary Cluster *(p102)*

Hang Roma *(p93)*

Humana Vintage *(p98)*

King Size *(p97)*

Mercato Esquilino *(p87)*

Panella *(p107)*

Pifebo *(p98)*

SiTenne *(p96)*

Tartufi dal Bosco *(p106)*

Trimani Enoteca *(p105)*

## A ARTS & CULTURE

Baths of Diocletian *(p112)*

Capitoline Museums *(p125)*

Colosseum *(p113)*

Domus Aurea *(p112)*

Domus Romane *(p114)*

Galleria d'Arte Moderna *(p128)*

Galleria Doria Pamphilj *(p117)*

Keats-Shelley Memorial House *(p117)*

Museum and Crypt of the Capuchin Friars *(p125)*

Trajan's Markets *(p114)*

Victor Emmanuel II Monument *(p119)*

## N NIGHTLIFE

The Barber Shop *(p151)*

Blackmarket Hall *(p154)*

The Court *(p141)*

Gatsby Cafè *(p152)*

The Race Club *(p150)*

Rome Opera House *(p144)*

## O OUTDOORS

Capitoline Hill *(p177)*

Esquiline Hill *(p178)*

Piazza della Madonna dei Monti *(p172)*

Piazza di Spagna *(p172)*

Piazza di Trevi *(p173)*

Quirinal Hill *(p178)*

Viminal Hill *(p177)*

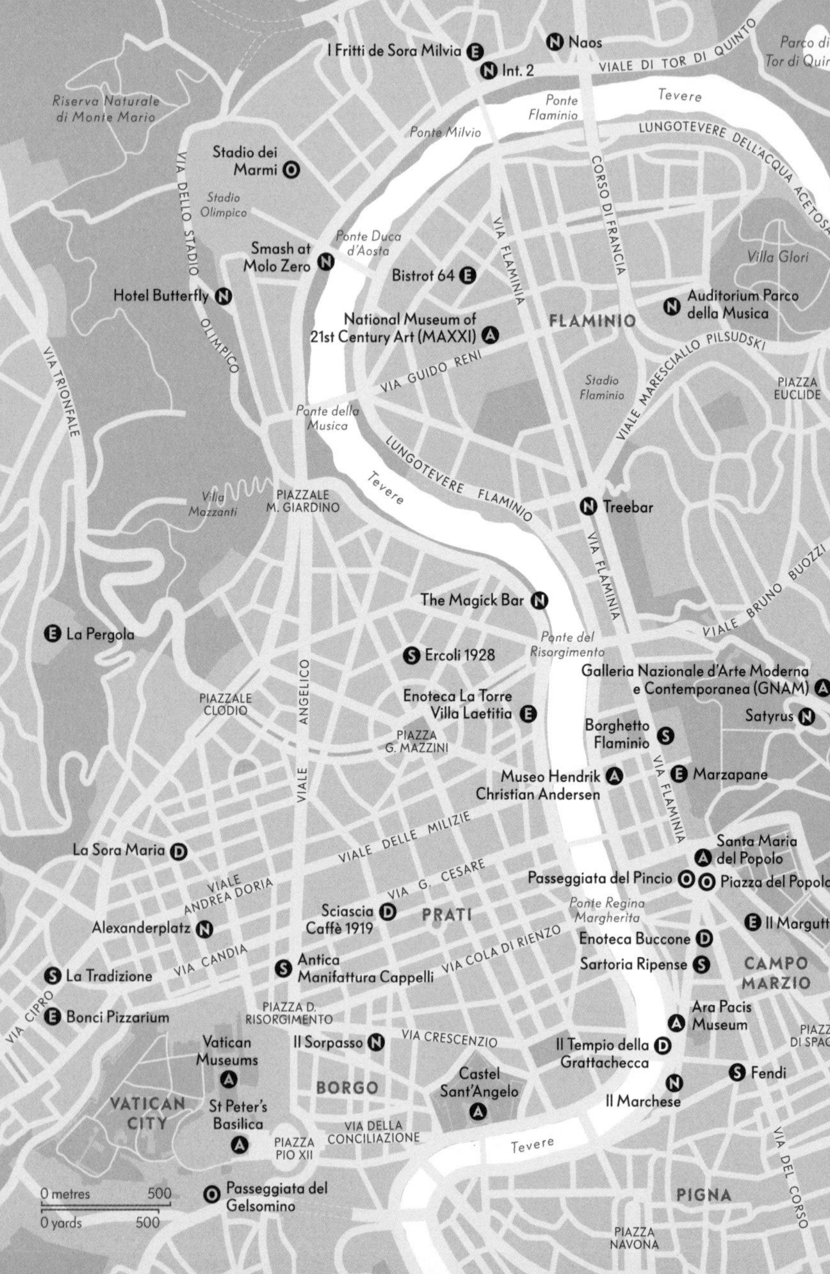
I Fritti de Sora Milvia
Naos
Int. 2
Viale di Tor di Quinto
Parco di Tor di Quint
Riserva Naturale di Monte Mario
Ponte Flaminio
Tevere
Ponte Milvio
Lungotevere dell'Acqua Acetosa
Stadio dei Marmi
Via dello Stadio Olimpico
Stadio Olimpico
Corso di Francia
Via Flaminia
Ponte Duca d'Aosta
Smash at Molo Zero
Bistrot 64
Villa Glori
Hotel Butterfly
Auditorium Parco della Musica
National Museum of 21st Century Art (MAXXI)
Flaminio
Viale Maresciallo Pilsudski
Via Trionfale
Via Guido Reni
Stadio Flaminio
Piazza Euclide
Ponte della Musica
Lungotevere Flaminio
Villa Mazzanti
Piazzale M. Giardino
Treebar
Viale Bruno Buozzi
The Magick Bar
La Pergola
Ponte del Risorgimento
Ercoli 1928
Galleria Nazionale d'Arte Moderna e Contemporanea (GNAM)
Viale Angelico
Piazzale Clodio
Enoteca La Torre Villa Laetitia
Satyrus
Borghetto Flaminio
Piazza G. Mazzini
Museo Hendrik Christian Andersen
Marzapane
Viale delle Milizie
La Sora Maria
Santa Maria del Popolo
Viale Andrea Doria
Via G. Cesare
Passeggiata del Pincio
Piazza del Popolo
Sciascia Caffè 1919
Prati
Ponte Regina Margherita
Il Margutta
Alexanderplatz
Via Cola di Rienzo
Enoteca Buccone
La Tradizione
Via Candia
Antica Manifattura Cappelli
Sartoria Ripense
Campo Marzio
Via Cipro
Bonci Pizzarium
Piazza D. Risorgimento
Ara Pacis Museum
Piazza di Spagna
Vatican Museums
Il Sorpasso
Via Crescenzio
Il Tempio della Grattachecca
Fendi
Castel Sant'Angelo
Borgo
Vatican City
St Peter's Basilica
Il Marchese
Via della Conciliazione
Piazza Pio XII
Via del Corso
0 metres 500
0 yards 500
Passeggiata del Gelsomino
Pigna
Piazza Navona

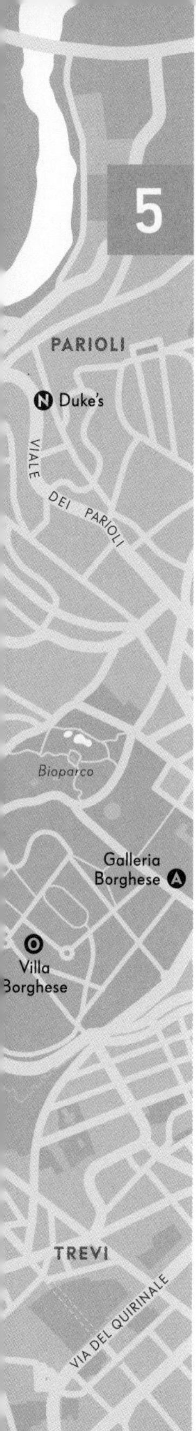


## EAT

Bistrot 64 *(p55)*

Bonci Pizzarium *(p44)*

Enoteca La Torre Villa Laetitia *(p53)*

I Fritti de Sora Milvia *(p32)*

Il Margutta *(p51)*

La Pergola *(p54)*

Marzapane *(p52)*

## DRINK

Enoteca Buccone *(p75)*

Il Tempio della Grattachecca *(p69)*

La Sora Maria *(p71)*

Sciascia Caffè 1919 *(p63)*

## SHOP

Antica Manifattura Cappelli *(p90)*

Borghetto Flaminio *(p85)*

Ercoli 1928 *(p106)*

Fendi *(p89)*

La Tradizione *(p104)*

Sartoria Ripense *(p90)*

## ARTS & CULTURE

Ara Pacis Museum *(p128)*

Castel Sant'Angelo *(p118)*

Galleria Borghese *(p116)*

Galleria Nazionale d'Arte Moderna e Contemporanea (GNAM) *(p116)*

National Museum of 21st Century Art (MAXXI) *(p131)*

Museo Hendrik Christian Andersen *(p127)*

Santa Maria del Popolo *(p118)*

St Peter's Basilica *(p118)*

Vatican Museums *(p124)*

## NIGHTLIFE

Alexanderplatz *(p145)*

Auditorium Parco della Musica *(p144)*

Duke's *(p142)*

Hotel Butterfly *(p155)*

Il Marchese *(p141)*

Il Sorpasso *(p142)*

Int. 2 *(p148)*

Naos *(p156)*

Satyrus *(p152)*

Smash at Molo Zero *(p157)*

The Magick Bar *(p154)*

Treebar *(p143)*

## OUTDOORS

Passeggiata del Gelsomino *(p167)*

Passeggiata del Pincio *(p164)*

Piazza del Popolo *(p173)*

Stadio dei Marmi *(p170)*

Villa Borghese *(p171)*

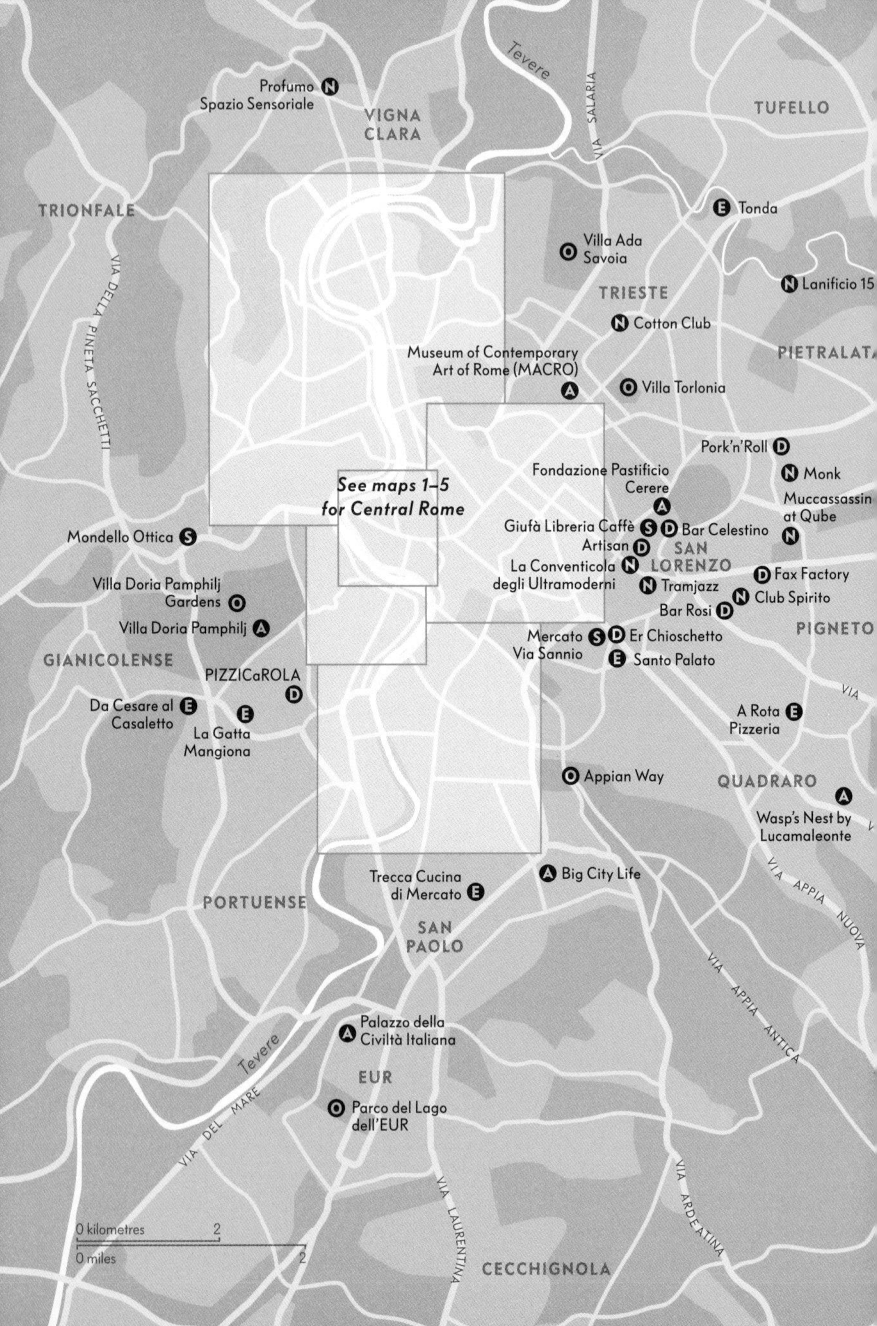

Tevere
VIA SALARIA
Profumo Spazio Sensoriale N
VIGNA CLARA
TUFELLO
TRIONFALE
E Tonda
O Villa Ada Savoia
N Lanificio 15
VIA DELLA PINETA SACCHETTI
TRIESTE
N Cotton Club
PIETRALATA
Museum of Contemporary Art of Rome (MACRO) A
O Villa Torlonia
Pork'n'Roll D
N Monk
Fondazione Pastificio Cerere A
Muccassassina at Qube N
See maps 1–5 for Central Rome
Mondello Ottica S
Giufà Libreria Caffè S
D Bar Celestino
Artisan D
SAN LORENZO
La Conventicola degli Ultramoderni N
D Fax Factory
N Tramjazz
N Club Spirito
Villa Doria Pamphilj Gardens O
Bar Rosi D
Villa Doria Pamphilj A
Mercato Via Sannio S
D Er Chioschetto
PIGNETO
GIANICOLENSE
E Santo Palato
PIZZICaROLA D
Da Cesare al Casaletto E
E La Gatta Mangiona
A Rota Pizzeria E
O Appian Way
QUADRARO
A Wasp's Nest by Lucamaleonte
A Big City Life
Trecca Cucina di Mercato E
PORTUENSE
SAN PAOLO
VIA APPIA NUOVA
VIA APPIA ANTICA
A Palazzo della Civiltà Italiana
Tevere
EUR
O Parco del Lago dell'EUR
VIA DEL MARE
VIA LAURENTINA
VIA ARDEATINA
0 kilometres 2
0 miles 2
CECCHIGNOLA

## E EAT



## D DRINK



## S SHOP



## A ARTS & CULTURE



## N NIGHTLIFE



## O OUTDOORS

# EAT

*In Rome, nothing starts a debate quite like food does. From where to find the best carbonara to the most digestible pizza dough (yes, really), everyone's got an opinion.*

# Street Food

***Pizza and fried bites are Roman staples, but nowadays you can also find traditional meals to go (or stuffed into bread). Locals love a quick and tasty snack, and nowhere does street food quite like it.***

## I FRITTI DE SORA MILVIA

**Map 5; Via Cassia 4, Ponte Milvio; ///themes.pirate.coining; www.ifrittidesoramilvia.it**

Heading to the Olympic stadium for a match? Then stopping by Sora Milvia's is a must. This institution is one of few *friggitorie,* where everything on offer is fried. Expect fish and most Roman classics: the *supplì all'amatriciana* (fried rice ball with tomato sauce and cured meat) and fried zucchini flowers are local heroes. There's usually a queue, so order ahead online to make it in time for kick-off.

## LEGS

**Map 3; Via Giovanni da Empoli, 23, Ostiense; ///zapped.handbook.highways; www.legs-roma.com**

Fried chicken reigns supreme at Legs. Place your order at the window and, moments later, you'll be digging into a succulent and crispy chicken thigh burger. Everything is served with a signature

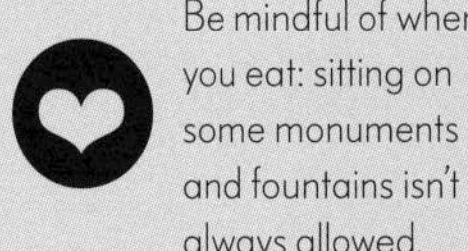


rosemary-infused sauce in a brioche bun from the Roscioli bakery. And be sure to wash it down with a craft beer – the selection here is one of the best in town.

## MORDI E VAI

**Map 3; Box 15, Mercato di Testaccio, Via Beniamino Franklin, Testaccio; ///belt.pounding.edicts; 347 663 2731**

This is probably Mercato di Testaccio's busiest stall, and it's all thanks to husband-and-wife team Sergio and Mara. Dishes like *allesso di scottona* (tender slow-cooked brisket) and oxtail stew are packed into rolls that Romans can't get enough of. Sadly, Sergio passed away in 2022, but his memory lives on at this stand, where you'll find the generously stuffed bites. Expect to make a mess.

» **Don't leave without** visiting Artenio at Box 90 to pick up a baked snack for later: loaves, mini pizzas, biscuits and *taralli* abound.

## FORNO CAMPO DE' FIORI

**Map 1; Campo de' Fiori 22, Campo de' Fiori; ///rattled.stay.humble; 06 6880 6662**

This historic bakery is a local favourite, meaning lunchtimes are hectic with passersby and workers alike piling in. Everyone's here for stuffed white pizza – the *pizza con la mortazza* (with mortadella) is perfection. Sneak a peek through the side door to see bakers lay out metres of pizza on repeat, and take note: there's a second branch on the left, so choose the one with the shortest wait.

## PASTIFICIO GUERRA

**Map 4; Via della Croce 8, Campo Marzio; ///sprays.drank.cupcake; 06 679 3102**

Wide-eyed tourists eyeing up the window displays on the luxe Via del Corso are oblivious to this budget lunch spot around the corner. Locals pop in for fresh, takeaway pasta – the menu changes daily, but it usually includes at least one classic option, like carbonara.

## SUPPLÌ

**Map 2; Via San Francesco a Ripa 137, Trastevere; ///props.probable.certified; www.suppliroma.it**

Known among locals as "Venanzio" after the owner, this place has been churning out *supplì* (deep-fried rice balls) since 1979. Classic variations with meat sauce and *rigaje* (chicken giblets) are made every day, while daily specials include *coda alla vaccinara* (oxtail sauce) and the seafood *moscardini supplì*. Still peckish? Top it off with a tasty slice of *pizza marinara al taglio*, a Roman classic.

» **Don't leave without** buying pecorino cheese for your own take on *cacio e pepe* from l'Antica Caciara next door.

## DAR FILETTARO

**Map 1; Largo dei Librari 88, Campo de' Fiori; ///outsiders.outsiders.twinge; 06 686 4018**

Yes, there's salami and mozzarella on the menu, but don't bother: you're here for the fish. This street food institution has served up battered and fried fillets of flaky *baccalà* (salt cod) to generations of

Romans since 1800. It's strictly accompanied by *puntarelle* (a bitter winter vegetable) and seasoned with garlic and anchovies. Enjoy with a glass of the house wine, or bring your own bottle for a fee.

## TRAPIZZINO

**Map 2; Piazza Trilussa 46, Trastevere; ///armful.mini.list; www.trapizzino.it**

Roman *pizzaiolo* (pizza chef) Stefano Callegari jump-started the street food revival in Rome with his *trapizzino* creation – a pizza pocket that takes inspiration from the *tramezzino* (a triangular sandwich that's served in bars). The crispy-on-the-outside, fluffy-on-the-inside dough is filled with Italian staples like chicken *cacciatore* (usually a hearty stew), aubergine *parmigiana* and *lingua* (tongue) in green sauce. Your mission? To eat one, then immediately another.

## BAR DEL CAPPUCCINO

**Map 1; Via Arenula 50, Jewish Quarter; ///iron.affords.monopoly; 06 6880 6042;**

Pairing your meal with a cappuccino may raise eyebrows in Italy, but not at Bar del Cappuccino (it's in the name, after all). Barista Luigi Santoro has famously served some of the best-decorated "latte art" cappuccinos for the last 50 years, before it was even a thing. Frothy coffees are paired, somewhat unexpectedly, with *pizza al taglio* filled with pastrami direct from Katz's Delicatessen in New York. The squares of pizza are served with homemade mayonnaise, pickles and a salad. Oh, and a cappuccino, for those so inclined.

# Sweet Treats

***In a city where it's customary to start the day with a coffee and pastry, it's only natural that every street has a temple to sweet treats, whether it's a*** **forno** ***(bakery),*** **pasticceria** ***(pastry shop) or*** **gelateria** ***(gelato shop).***

## GELATERIA FASSI

**Map 4; Via Principe Eugenio 65, Esquilino; ///costumes.radio.crawling; www.gelateriafassi.com**

Welcome to one of the best *gelaterie* in Rome – nay, Italy. Andrea Fassi is the fifth generation to run this century-old shop, having learned from his forefathers the millimetric precision that the irresistible dessert requires. We recommend you try the gelato master's perfect pistachio flavour: pale in colour, naturally creamy and with a slightly salty aftertaste. The proof of the pudding really is in the eating.

## TORCÈ

**Map 3; Viale Aventino 5, Aventine; ///reclaim.rankings.spilled; www.gelateriatorce.it**

Carrot, celery, gorgonzola cheese, spicy *habanero*: these are not your run-of-the-mill gelato flavours. But, mamma mia, are they delicious. Owner Claudio Torcè made his name showcasing Rome

Romans are fair and friendly so, if you're unsure of gelato flavours, ask to sample ahead of ordering.

and the surrounding region's best ingredients in the form of gelato. Forget the classics; it's worth being adventurous and sampling an unusual flavour or two.

## FORNO BOCCIONE

**Map 1; Via del Portico d'Ottavia 1, Jewish Quarter; ///bottled.bubble.other; 06 687 8637**

For decades, Forno Boccione has been making traditional Jewish-Roman pastries, like almond *crostate* (tarts) and *ginetti* biscuits, just right for dunking in a morning cappuccino. While you try to choose just one or two treats to take home, chat to lively owner Mrs Vilma, who knows every age-old recipe by heart.

» **Don't leave without** asking for a slice of the ricotta and sour cherry pie – it's one of the kosher bakery's traditional recipes.

## PASTICCERIA REGOLI

**Map 4; Via dello Statuto 60, Esquilino; ///sport.chief.copying; www.pasticceriaregoli.com**

Rome's sweetest treat, *maritozzo* dates back to the 18th century when, legend says, suitors would hide an engagement ring inside the bun's whipped cream for their intended to find (*maritozzo* comes from *marito*, which means husband). Whether you're planning to pop the question or just sate your sweet tooth, Regoli is the place to sample this fluffy, cream-stuffed brioche. The bakery makes hundreds every day, always served with a smile from the gentlemen at the counter.

## OTALEG

**Map 2; Via di San Cosimato 14a, Trastevere; ///pursuit.useful.engine; 338 651 5450**

The queue that snakes out the door of this tiny *gelateria* is evidence of its fan base. Flavours range from the traditional (think pistachio, coffee, fruit sorbets) to the creative, like *cacio e pepe*, honey and walnut, and whatever gelato master Marco Radicioni has come up with that day.

» **Don't leave without** trying the *pesche tabacchiera*, if it's available. Made with sweet doughnut peaches, this is the perfect summery gelato.

## GREZZO RAW CHOCOLATE

**Map 4; Via Urbana 130, Monti; ///wonderfully.soothing.swung; www.grezzorawchocolate.com**

This *cioccolateria's* cute-looking truffles and little potted chocolate desserts are the perfect finish after dinner out in Monti. All ingredients used are vegan, gluten-free and certified organic, so there's something for everyone. We'll have a dark chocolate gelato, thanks.

## GIOLITTI

**Map 3; Via Amerigo Vescpucci 35, Testaccio; ///sliders.matter.reaction; www.giolitti.it**

Don't trust online opening hours; the staff of Giolitti open when they want. What began as a *cremeria* (milk shop) in the 1800s has grown into a trio of *gelaterie*, but it's the Testaccio branch that feels the most unchanged. It's here that you can hope to taste the secret *zabaione* (custard) flavour, which is given to the most deserving (so be polite).

## Liked by the locals

**"Ice cream parlours are the real neighbourhood churches. It's in Rome's *gelaterie* that everyone is equal and equally happy. There're no other establishments in Rome like them."**

CARLA D'AMBROSIO, OWNER OF IL CAPRICCIO DI CARLA GELATERIA, PIGNETO

# Charming Trattorias

***Ask any Roman where they're happiest and they'll say at a trattoria. Serving comforting fare in a familiar surrounding, some places are so tried and tested that regulars don't even need a menu.***

## DA CESARE AL CASALETTO

**Map 6; Via del Casaletto 45, Monteverde; ///playoffs.remarks.withdraw; www.trattoriadacesare.it**

Is there anything more Italian than enjoying a long, lingering meal on a vine-draped patio? That's exactly how it's done at Da Cesare. Ordering every course is ideal, but the *primi* (first courses) – like the *amatriciana* and a killer carbonara – are what locals love. Don't neglect the fried antipasti either, like the deep-fried gnocchi atop a *cacio e pepe* sauce.

## SANTO PALATO

**Map 6; Piazza Tarquinia 4 a/b, Esquilino; ///stormed.ship.kitten; 067 720 7354**

Chef Sarah Cicolini hails from Abruzzo but is known in the Italian capital for her take on Roman cuisine. She makes the most of every part of the animal, both as tradition dictates and with the aim of tackling food waste. Classic offal-based dishes are on the menu here, often with a fresh take, like the stand-out breaded oxtail meatball served alongside a lovage and peanut sauce. The dishes offer familiar comfort with a modern twist, and are best enjoyed with wine, bread and the chatter of friends at the table.

## CHECCHINO DAL 1887

**Map 3; Via di Monte Testaccio 30, Testaccio; ///tailors.logs.skinny; www.checchino-dal-1887.com**

If anywhere encapsulates the Italian art of *cenetta tranquilla* – a long, heart-warming dinner with loved ones – it's Checchino dal 1887. This is one of the oldest trattorias in the city, where four generations of the Mariani family have served traditional Roman cuisine for over a century. Offal is the speciality: the classic *coda alla vaccinara* (stuffed veal tail in tomato sauce) was first made here.

» **Don't leave without** politely asking the waiter to show you the wine cellar, made with ancient Roman amphoras.

## AL POMPIERE

**Map 1; Via di Santa Maria dei Calderari 38, Jewish Quarter; ///keeps.madness.curvy; www.alpompiereroma.com**

Anniversary around the corner? Book a table at Al Pompiere, set in a former Baroque palace (ask for a table upstairs to enjoy the original ceiling frescoes). If you're lucky, the friendly waiter Mauro will be available to give great food recommendations and tell stories that date back to the trattoria's opening in the 1900s.

# Solo, Pair, Crowd

**A trattoria is the perfect place to experience home-style Italian cooking. Pull up a chair, no matter the size of your party.**

## FLYING SOLO

### Wine and dine yourself

Enjoying a meal alone in Rome is a must. Find a table at Sora Lella's on Isola Tiberina and indulge in a full meal, complete with pasta and desert. This typical trattoria is run by the eponymous founder's nephews.

## IN A PAIR

### Pasta for two

Treat your date to dinner at Luciano Cucina Italiana, where talented chef Luciano whips up the most incredible carbonara.

## FOR A CROWD

### Find a large table

When friends are visiting from out of town, book a table at Giggetto, near Campo de' Fiori. This place pours wine with a generous hand and makes an excellent fried artichoke. Your friends won't want to leave.

## TRECCA CUCINA DI MERCATO

**Map 6; Via Alessandro Severo 220, Ostiense; ///dining.boasted.tennis; www.trecca.superbexperience.com**

Nothing beats grandma's cooking. At least that's the philosophy at this spot, run by the Trecastelli brothers, Niccolò and Manuel. Head over for Sunday lunch and enjoy *amatriciana* pasta served in a salad bowl, a nod to how their *nonna* would serve it at home.

## LA TAVERNACCIA DA BRUNO

**Map 3; Via Giovanni da Castel Bolognese 63, Trastevere; ///pleasing.upper.blurts; www.latavernacciaroma.com**

This family-run trattoria is in the hands of Paola and Patrizia Persiani, daughters of the restaurant's namesake, who opened the place in 1968. Rustic, home-style cooking from Rome and Umbria is on the menu: slow-cooked meats and stews, fresh pastas slathered in sauce, and rich platters of cured meats and cheese.

» **Don't leave without** ordering the suckling pig. Cooked in a wood-fired oven, this umami-loaded roast pork satisfies primal urges.

## TRATTORIA DA AUGUSTO

**Map 2; Vicolo de' Renzi 15, Trastevere; ///nursery.mostly.cashier; 06 580 3798**

In true trattoria style, the menu at Da Augusto changes daily and has done so for the last 50 years. Regulars, though, know that great *gnocchi* is always on Thursdays and *rigatoni con la pajata* on Tuesdays. There's almost always a queue, but it's worth the wait.

# Perfect Pizzerias

***Here in Italy, pizza generally falls into two camps: thin and crispy, or chewy with a thicker crust. You'll hear locals adamantly declare their favourite, but we say don't buy into the rivalry – there's room for both.***

## BONCI PIZZARIUM

**Map 5; Via della Meloria 43, Prati; ///enacted.speeding.small; www.bonci.it/pizzarium**

Gabriele Bonci, of *Chef's Table* fame, serves the tastiest *pizza al trancio* you'll ever eat. The large, rectangular pizzas are sold by the slice and draw a crowd – on one side of the doors you'll find the inevitable queue and on the other groups chomping down on their coveted slices. Bonci's Roman-style, potato-topped option is a carby nirvana not to be missed.

## 180 GRAMMI

**Map 6; Via Genazzano 32, Centocelle; ///pools.indicate.guards; www.180gpizzeriaromana.com**

Getting to 180 Grammi in Rome's eastern suburbs can be a trek, especially on Rome's notoriously plodding public transport, but it's well worth it. Pizza chef Jacopo Mercuro's process is meticulous, employing an extra-long leavening process for a crispy, chewy dough and topping it with quality ingredients. He clearly has a lot of fun too, coming up with creative combinations like the menu special "Pineapple Express", which is topped with mozzarella, *guanciale*, an *angostura* and mustard gel, plus – God forbid – pineapple.

**» Don't leave without trying the *supplì ubriaco*, a "drunk" fried rice ball made with local porchetta and a generous pour of white wine.**

## A ROTA PIZZERIA

**Map 6; Via di Tor Pignattara 190, Pigneto; ///hacking.unity.such; 345 547 9532**

The pizzas at A Rota are so incredibly good that you'll be back for more (fittingly, *a rota* means "to get addicted"). Italian-Egyptian pizza chef Sami El Sabawi studied the art of pizza-making from grand master Gabriele Bonci *(p44)* and, like his teacher, he prefers to craft a small and exclusive menu. Our favourite? It's got to be the Crostino, topped with mozzarella and prosciutto.

## SEU ILLUMINATI

**Map 3; Via Angelo Bargoni 10, Monteverde; ///props.soulful.pounds; www.seupizza.com**

"In pizza we trust", the neon lights of Seu Illuminati read – and were wiser words ever written? Romans live by the pizzeria's motto, celebrating the arrival of the weekend at this trendy joint. Toppings are taken seriously, with a mix of traditional and creative, while the dough is double-leavened and super soft.

## AI MARMI

**Map 2; Viale di Trastevere 53, Trastevere; ///cloak.pricier.small; 06 580 0919**

The scene inside this pizzeria is something to behold: maestros by the oven make pizza and *supplì* (fried rice balls) at the speed of light, while waiters whiz to and fro delivering multiple plates at a time to hungry patrons. Above it all, a large old-school lightbox shows the menu, unchanged since the 1970s – it's all about Roman-style pizza here, thin and with a crunch.

» **Don't leave without** adding the Tuscan *fagioli all'uccelletto* (a bean and tomato dish) to your order, perfect alongside your pizza.

## LA MONTECARLO

**Map 1; Vicolo Savelli 13, Piazza Navona; ///usual.spreads.graphic; www.lamontecarlo.it**

If you're after a pizza so big no plate can contain it, head to La Montecarlo, a stone's throw from the ever-bustling Piazza Navona. Keep an eye out for the tongue-in-cheek honours by the door, including a self-awarded "Michelin" star.

## LA GATTA MANGIONA

**Map 6; Via Ozanam 30, Monteverde; ///breath.giggled.prepare; www.lagattamangiona.com**

Where else could you find not one but seven types of pizza margherita? That's La Gatta Mangiona, the first gourmet (and, somewhat randomly, cat-themed) pizzeria in Rome. Creativity is at the heart of the menu, where versions of a staple recipe like margherita pizza are reinvented with different cheeses, spicy sauces and even fusion flavours. The doughy offerings are perhaps more Neapolitan than Roman in their origins, but no one's complaining: locals keep coming back for more.

## TONDA

**Map 6; Via Valle Corteno 31, Monte Sacro; ///skins.split.writers; 06 818 0960**

Come to Tonda prepared to do some serious eating. Founder Stefano Callegari really knows food – after all, he invented the *trapizzino (p35)*. Pizza is the main event, but you won't want to miss the mouth-watering fried *supplì* either. From classics to the daily specials, with fillings like chicory and *'nduja* (spicy sausage), each one is a masterpiece. They're the perfect prelude to the creative Neapolitan-style pizzas on offer, including the local favourite: a *cacio e pepe* pizza, made using ice. And, for fans looking for a fix, the beloved *trapizzino* is also on the menu.

### Try it!
### PIZZA-MAKING CLASS

After sampling all of the pizza in Rome, it's hard to part ways with it. Head to the Rome Pizza School *(www.romepizzaschool.com)* to try your hand at pizza-making and impress your friends at home.

# Veggie and Vegan

***There's no denying Roman cuisine is meat-heavy at times, but there are plenty of veggie-friendly classics. Fried artichokes, sautéed chicory and tasty pastas are mainstays that no Roman can get enough of.***

## MARIGOLD

**Map 3; Via Giovanni da Empoli 37, Ostiense; ///parent.snores.mergers; www.marigoldroma.com**

Breakfast is usually light in Rome – locals tend to graze on a *cornetto* with their cappuccino – but early birds craving something more are well served by this microbakery. Danish baker Sofie and her Italian husband Domenico whip up great veggie breakfasts, like Sicilian avocado on rye bread, decadent buttermilk pancakes and satisfying shakshuka (big, flaky pastries also come as standard).

## RIFUGIO ROMANO

**Map 4; Via Volturno 39/41, Esquilino; ///props.fines.prompt; www.rifugioromano.com**

No one has to miss out on the pure joy of cheese-laden pasta or a creamy panna cotta. Serving vegan alternatives of practically every Roman dish, Rifugio Romano gives those old-school Roman vibes you've read about. Tuck into some *spaghetti alla carbonara, cacio e pepe, supplì* (fried rice balls) and even cold cut platters – all plant-based, and no less delicious.

## AROMATICUS

**Map 4; Via Urbana 134, Monti; ///become.heat.piglet; www.aromaticus-roma.com**

Eating at Aromaticus is a restorative experience: there's a warm home-away-from-home vibe, with tables surrounded by aromatic plants and edible flowers. Then there's the almost fully vegan menu, featuring soups, creative salads, pastas, tasty wraps, fresh juices and kombucha. A lunch or dinner here will ground anyone looking for respite away from the bustle of the city centre.

**» Don't leave without trying the vegan tiramisù, a super tasty dairy-free version of the beloved Italian desert.**

Looking for a break from the hubbub of cars, tourists and Vespas? Rustic I Casali del Pino is the place to go *(www.icasalidelpino.it)*. This organic farm houses a B&B and restaurant designed by Anna Fendi Venturini. The menu has lots of veggie options: the fresh, homemade *caciotta* cheese, made with vegetable rennet, is especially popular among vegetarians. We recommend asking for a picnic basket and heading out into the Parco di Veio, where the B&B is located.

# Solo, Pair, Crowd

**From sweet snacks to filling meals, there are plenty of places to enjoy veggie food, no matter who you're with.**

## FLYING SOLO

### Table for one

Hungry after a morning stroll through the historic centre? Écru, located right next to the Victor Emmanuel II bridge, offers a completely vegan, gluten-free and raw menu. Order a chia pudding bowl, grab a window seat and plan the rest of your day.

## IN A PAIR

### Picnic in the park

Buy a picnic basket from Vivi Bistrot in Villa Pamphilj and take your pal for a stroll in the park. Enjoy the fresh juices, healthy bites (many of them veggie) and delicious cakes.

## FOR A CROWD

### A vegan feast

Looking to fill up before heading out with the group? At Ops!, close to Porta Pia, you'll find a diverse, completely vegan fresh buffet with something for everyone.

## ROMEOW CAT BISTROT

**Map 3; Via Francesco Negri 15, Ostiense; ///divider.spare.zones; www.romeowcatbistrot.com**

Yes, there are a couple of resident cats here but, in our opinion, the real reason to visit this cat café is the incredible all-vegan menu. Many of the desserts are even raw and gluten-free. You can't really go wrong with any of the vegan takes on Italian classics or the more experimental signature dishes, but the cheesecake is a must-try.

## MATER TERRAE

**Map 1; Largo Febo 2, Piazza Navona; ///divider.speaker.flatten; www.biohotelraphael.com**

Mater Terrae serves up vegetarian dining *par excellence*. Come prepared to feast on expertly made dishes, such as the artichoke cream with parsley mint mousse and roasted chestnuts. It has a great location to boot: head up for an early dinner to catch sight glowing sunset over the Piazza Navona.

## IL MARGUTTA

**Map 5; Via Margutta 118, Campo Marzio; ///beast.under.paddock; www.ilmargutta.bio**

Artsy and quirky restaurant Il Margutta has been the go-to place for Rome's vegetarians since 1979. Arrive expecting classics with a twist (like the *amatriciana* pasta dish), vegan cheese platters and great desserts. Even better: most of the dishes are made with organic, locally sourced ingredients.

# Special Occasion

***Whether you're celebrating a birthday, anniversary or payday, Rome knows how to make you feel like a god. Expect palazzo-style settings, convivial waiters and the most incredible food in the country.***

## MARZAPANE

**Map 5; Via Flaminia 64, Flaminio; ///offshore.brands.work; www.marzapaneroma.com**

It's all about mixing Italian and Spanish flavours at Marzapane, a chic dining room in artsy Flaminio. Those feeling flush book a seat at the ultra-exclusive Chef's Table, by the kitchen, where chefs freestyle dishes before talking patrons through each creation. For us mere mortals, the three-course lunch menu is a delicious – and affordable – alternative.

## SALUMERIA ROSCIOLI

**Map 1; Via dei Giubbonari 21, Campo de' Fiori; ///deserved.trainers.cobble; www.salumeriaroscioli.com**

We have the local Roscioli family to thank for this food nirvana. What began as a family-run bakery in the 1970s has become an institution, where loved ones raise glasses of prosecco on high days and holidays. Part deli, part trattoria, the place has all the vibes of a gourmet restaurant without any of the pretension. Choose from the wall lined with bottles of *vino* before sharing plates of artichokes and truffled burrata. As for your *primo* (first course) and *secondo* (second course), carbonara followed by sea bass is just the ticket on any occasion.

**» Don't leave without** gifting yourself a copy of *Roscioli: The bread, the kitchen and Rome*. The book tells the story of the food-loving Roman family and includes 30 of their most popular recipes to try at home.

## ENOTECA LA TORRE VILLA LAETITIA

**Map 5; Lungotevere delle Armi 23, Prati; ///rafters.pulsing.mixture; www.enotecalatorreroma.com**

When Romans want a special moment, they head here. The southern Italian menu is wonderful, but the setting is to die for: a Baroque-style villa replete with chandeliers and marble pillars (fashion designer Anna Fendi Venturini actually lives here). We recommend a lunch booking, when the light shines through the enormous arched windows and you can see the garden beyond.

## ZIA RESTAURANT

**Map 2; Via Goffredo Mameli 45, Trastevere; ///crusted.explains.transmitted; www.ziarestaurant.com**

Trastevere locals have their pick of traditional trattorias but, when a big anniversary or promotion warrants something a bit fancier, they book a table at Zia. The restaurant's modern French-Italian menu keeps patrons sighing with satisfaction from the first to the final dish. And to the last glass – this place has a fantastic wine selection.

## RETROBOTTEGA

**Map 1; Via della Stelletta 4, Campo Marzio; ///boomed.fairness.javelin; www.retro-bottega.com**

You certainly don't need to dress up for this place, the coolest of Rome's gourmet restaurants. Industrial chic in style, Retrobottega is all about returning to simpler, more humble times, when vegetables were at the centre of family meals. Chef Alessandro forages in the Lazio region's hills and along its coastline for herbs, berries and veg to inspire his rustic menu. Of course, a glass of something is needed for a celebratory toast; any one of Retrobottega's natural wines forms the perfect accompaniment to a foraged feast.

» **Don't leave without** practising the Italian joy of *scarpetta* – making your bread into a "little shoe" and sopping up any delicious sauces left on your plate.

## LA PERGOLA

**Map 5; Via Cadlolo 101, Trionfale; ///ruby.scarcely.suitable; www.romecavalieri.com**

Every Roman hopes to eat at La Pergola at least once in their lifetime. On the top floor of the Waldorf Astoria, the city's most luxurious restaurant is an extravaganza of oil paintings, creaseless white tablecloths and floral displays, though it's the sweeping views of the Eternal City that are impossible to tear your gaze from. The menu is likewise a spectacle, thanks to three-Michelin-starred chef Heinz Beck. His dishes are sublime, with choices like fennel risotto topped with scallops and venison on a bed of lentils. As for drinks, there are 30,000 bottles in the restaurant's wine cellar and 55 types

No jeans or trainers here – this place is fancy. Didn't pack a blazer? Pergola has some spares to hand.

of water to choose from. Even a herbal tea comes with a dash of opulence; your waiter will wheel out a trolley of herbs and snip your chosen foliage tableside.

## PIPERO

**Map 1; Corso Vittorio Emanuele II 250, Regola; ///employ.safe.message; www.piperoroma.it**

There are two reasons to book a table for your big day at Pipero. Firstly, owner and *maître* Alessandro is the perfect host. He knows exactly what you want, when you want it, and will go out of his way to make your celebration that extra bit special. Secondly, the creative Jewish-Roman cuisine whipped up by chef Ciro Scamardella. Take his delicious rendition of carbonara, which Alessandro will recommend you order *after* dessert; it really is the perfect finish to your meal.

## BISTROT 64

**Map 5; Via Calderini 64, Flaminio; ///fresh.looked.partner; www.bistrot64.it**

If you watched Stanley Tucci's *Searching for Italy*, you'll be familiar with Noda Kotaro, the Japanese chef making waves in Rome with his sensational *cacio e pepe*. Though the vibe at this bistro is posh, and the menu leans toward haute cuisine, the prices are happily affordable; the tasting menu (which includes the option of Noda's famous *cacio e pepe*) is just €70 per head. Surely there's no better way to mark an occasion than by following in Stanley's footsteps?

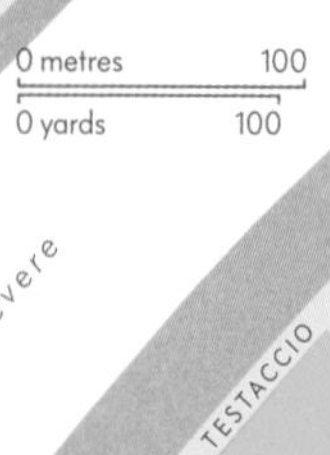


**Stop for a pick-me-up at**
**PASTICCERIA LINARI**

Order an espresso and, if you're not full, a *maritozzo* – a traditional Roman pastry loaded with whipped cream. This place is famous for them. 3

2 **Join a**
**TASTE OF TESTACCIO TOUR**

Discover the best gourmet shops and stalls in Testaccio with the help of a guide, sampling balsamic vinegar, cheese and prosciutto as you explore. At the end of the tour you'll make a *bruschetta al pomodoro*.

**Stock up on goodies at**
**MERCATO DI TESTACCIO**

Thanks to the foodie tour, which stops at the market, you'll know exactly which stalls to revisit for delicious delicacies to take home. 4

***Monte Testaccio*** *is actually an artificial mound made up of 53 million broken olive oil amphorae discarded by the Romans.*

*In the 1900s, streets were planned in a grid around the slaughter-house that today houses modern art museum* ***Mattatoio****.*

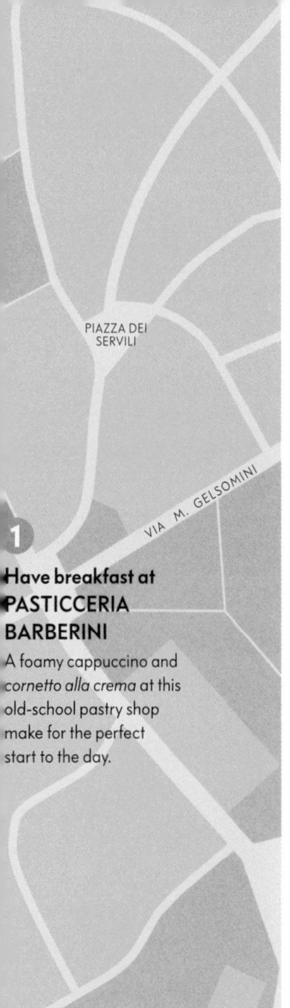




# A foodie morning in **Testaccio**

South of the historic centre, Testaccio is known by locals as "the heart of Rome". Why? Well, this humble patch has been vital to the city for millennia; it was a key trade hub in the Roman Empire and later the meatpacking district in the 19th century. Today, this is the real Rome: a down-to-earth village in a metropolis, home to families that have lived here for generations and a food scene that celebrates its heritage. Nowhere embodies this more than the market, where locals shop – just as their relatives did years ago.

**1. Pasticceria Barberini**
Via Marmorata 41; www.pasticceriabarberini.it
///spinning.lives.minute

**2. Taste of Testaccio Tour**
Piazza Testaccio 41; www.eatingeurope.com/rome/taste-of-testaccio
///unroll.fitter.encoder

**3. Pasticceria Linari**
Via Nicola Zabaglia 9; www.pasticcerialinari.com
///recline.meant.fended

**4. Mercato di Testaccio**
Via Aldo Manuzio; www.mercatoditestaccio.it
///definite.powerful.junior

**Monte Testaccio**
*///coarser.loaded.solo*

**Mattatoio**
*///thus.leopard.boarding*

# DRINK

*There's nothing more Italian than sipping a cappuccino, craft beer or glass of wine while indulging in* dolce far niente *– the sweet art of doing nothing.*

# Coffee Shops

***Romans live on coffee, caffeinating three, four or five times a day. The ritual tends to take place at the counter, where locals catch up with their neighbours over the sound of clinking crockery and hissing steam.***

## TRAM DEPOT

**Map 3; Via Marmorata 13, Testaccio; ///allows.instance.swelling**

This vintage tram carriage turned tiny coffee kiosk is stationed by a busy intersection in Testaccio and yet, in spite of the constant hum of passing traffic, it feels like a little slice of calm. Under the shade of trees, locals chatter at the cluster of little tables, cradling their artisanal coffees made with beans sourced from small-batch roasters. The only snag? There's no bathroom.

## FARO

**Map 4; Via Piave 55, Salario; ///poodle.point.enhancement; www.farorome.com**

Unlike a lot of cafés in Italy, where coffee is drank swiftly at the counter, you're encouraged to sit down and linger over the speciality brews at Faro. Here, the roasting is lighter and more delicate than usual so try your coffee without sugar (although

An espresso enjoyed standing at the bar tends to cost €1–1.50; it'll cost more if you sit at a table.

you'll still see Italians enthusiastically pouring sugar into their coffee) to really get the full flavour profile. This is the place to sip and savour.

## GRAN CAFFÈ RIONE VIII

**Map 1; Via di Santa Maria del Pianto 59, Jewish Quarter; ///otters.purple.wing; 068 675 0067**

Wine bottles are arranged to the rafters in this cavernous café-bar but rest assured, it does a great cappuccino. Mornings are busy, with long-timers debating heatedly over their newspapers and pals meeting for pre-work espressos. Find a spare seat near the counter and enjoy people-watching with your coffee.

**» Don't leave without** checking out the selection of Italian chocolates and panettone – ideal gifts for your loved ones back home (or yourself).

## TAZZA D'ORO

**Map 1; Via degli Orfani 84, Piazza Navona; ///broccoli.showed.shelters; www.tazzadorocoffeeshop.com**

Kitted out with marble countertops, wood panelling and burnished fittings, this old-school coffee shop (found just a few steps from the Pantheon) threw open its doors in 1944. Beans are imported from Central and South America and roasted on site, making it a *torrefazione* (roastery) as well as a coffee shop. It's hardly a secret, with tourists and locals alike piling in for a coffee and to stock up on beans to take home.

## FAX FACTORY

**Map 6; Via Raimondi 87, Pigneto; ///wire.them.tonight; www.faxfactory.it**

It's part sceney café, part communal workspace at this Pigneto outpost. Caffeinated writers tap furiously at their laptops, remote workers natter with owners Luca and Gaia as they sip their V60 drip coffees and, when *aperitivo* hour rolls around, DJs start spinning vinyl.

**» Don't leave without checking out the café's art exhibitions, which celebrate local talent. You might find something for your own walls.**

## CAFFÈ SANT'EUSTACHIO

**Map 1; Piazza di Sant'Eustachio 82, Piazza Navona; ///january.flying.stone; www.caffesanteustachio.com**

Handily placed halfway between Piazza Navona and the Pantheon, this little spot is the ultimate Roman coffee shop. The café has been serving the city's best Arabica blends and froth-topped coffees since 1938. What's its secret? To this day, no one

Is there anything more Italian than sipping an espresso in the company of Neo-Classical statues? We think not. Tucked away in the studio of 19th-century sculptor Antonio Canova, Caffè Canova *(Via del Babuino 150a)* is jam-packed with life-size saints and busts of scowling politicians – you'll feel their gaze as you sit at the café tables. Prefer not to be watched? It's fine to drink your espresso at the counter, too.

knows; the barmen cleverly turn their backs when preparing an order. Of course, you can stand up at the counter to sip your coffee and try to catch a glimpse of the secret technique, but we recommend paying a couple more euros to sit outside. It's here that all Roman life is on display; you might even spot Gucci's design mogul Alessandro Michele swinging by for his daily espresso.

## ANTICO CAFFÈ GRECO

**Map 4; Via dei Condotti 86, Campo Marzio; ///glare.firmly.amid; www.anticocaffegreco.eu**

What do Casanova, Buffalo Bill and Elizabeth Taylor have in common? They've all had a coffee at this place, Italy's second-oldest café (it opened in 1760). A sense of history awaits around every corner here, thanks to the café's countless oil paintings, suited waiters and plush velvet seating (one sofa belonged to Hans Christian Andersen, who lived upstairs). Neighboured by Prada and Cartier, this is where Romans take anyone they're looking to impress. And we mean *really* impress – an espresso costs a whopping €7.

## SCIASCIA CAFFÈ 1919

**Map 5; Via Fabio Massimo 80a, Prati; ///skewed.petted.tone; www.sciasciacaffe1919.it**

"To be good, coffee must be black as night, hot as hell and sweet as love." So goes the saying at Sciascia. And the coffee shop certainly ticks all the boxes with its signature *caffè con cioccolato* – an espresso poured over a dollop of melted chocolate that lines the cup.

# Local Bars

***Rome's long-standing bars testify to the local love of whiling away the hours in a welcoming setting, drink in hand. It's in these timeless spots that you'll find true Roman hospitality.***

## BAR FARNESE

**Map 1; Via dei Baullari 20, Parione; ///rush.prawn.proceeds; 06 686 1816**

Looking to channel your inner Gregory Peck or Audrey Hepburn? Bar Farnese perfectly captures the Rome of the 1950s, with its fading photographs, vintage signage and waistcoated staff. Call in for a coffee and chat about the weather (if your Italian's up to it) with charming Mr Angelo – the fifth generation to run this iconic bar. Once you've finished and said your ciaos, do as the locals do and stock up on produce at nearby Mercato di Campo de' Fiori *(p85)*.

## LA BOTTEGA DEL CAFFÈ

**Map 4; Piazza della Madonna dei Monti 5, Monti; ///survivor.tasty.walnuts; 06 474 1578**

This one's the poshest on the list so, yes, the drinks are a tad pricier, but with good reason. Tucked away in genteel Monti, the bar's bougainvillea-draped terrace sits pretty in a cobblestone piazza.

This is the spot to sit back and relax of an afternoon, sipping a cocktail to the trickling soundtrack of the square's fountain. Can life be more beautiful?

**» Don't leave without** crossing the piazza to the ivy-covered Via della Madonna dei Monti, once home to Michelangelo.

## BAR GIANICOLO

**Map 2; Piazzale Aurelio 5, Monteverde; ///composers.cookies.magnets; 06 580 6275**

Crowning Janiculum Hill, this simple little bar occupies the spot where, in the 1860s, General Garibaldi tried to conquer Rome in order to unify Italy. Things are more chilled these days, thanks largely to bar owner Bandaro (so-called because he wears a bandana *all* the time), who provides banter and beers rather than war-mongering cries. In need of some shade? Or seeking refuge from the rain? There's a drink waiting for you at Bar Gianicolo – Bandaro will see to it.

## BAR CELESTINO

**Map 6; Via degli Ausoni 62, San Lorenzo; ///rewarded.those.elbow; 065 272 6438**

Thanks largely to the university located here, San Lorenzo is a hotbed of street art, flourishing bookshops and free thinking, and this LGBTQ+ hangout lies at its heart. A lot has changed in the area since the bar first opened its doors back in 1904, but it still remains a firm local favourite. Want proof? Look no further than the crowds mingling outside, sipping beers.

## BAR ROSI

**Map 6; Via del Pigneto 117, Pigneto; ///copiers.wanted.endings; 380 908 0195**

Things have little changed at this fabled bar since it opened in 1970. The same brown cups and saucers line the counter, Italian starlets still smoulder from their picture frames, and members of the Rosi family continue to serve coffees and *aperitivi* with a smile. Poet and director Pier Paolo Pasolini was a regular here in his time, and it feels as if he could walk through the door at any moment.

## BAR DEL FICO

**Map 1; Piazza del Fico 26, Piazza Navona; ///firms.jets.replace; www.bardelfico.com**

Outside Bar del Fico, under the shade of an ancient fig tree (*fico* means fig), you'll see *nonni* playing intense games of chess. At the call of "check-mate", the players wander into the shabby-chic bar, debriefing on the game over a couple of beers.  Why not join them?

## BAR SAN CALISTO

**Map 2; Piazza di San Calisto 3, Trastevere; ///rooms.code.miracle; www.barsancalisto.it**

Dirt-cheap and cheerful, this typically Italian bar is an institution – it's hard to imagine Rome without it. Why? Well, for years it's run like clockwork. From 10am, regulars swing by for a coffee or cheeky gelato. Then, with the arrival of *aperitivo* hour, groups of friends arrive for a livener, animatedly toasting negronis and making conversation with

After a drink, walk up to the Acqua Paola fountain. Sure, it's steep but the views are worth the hike.

those at the table next to them. A word to the wise: there's no table service here so you'll need to order at the counter inside and return with your receipt to settle up.

## CAFFÈ TEVERE

**Map 3; Largo Giovanni Battista Marzi 7, Testaccio; ///monkeys.prefix.sizzled; 065 728 5291**

On any given evening, you'll likely find a clutch of locals enjoying an Aperol spritz or glass of wine under the neon lights of Caffè Tevere, grateful to unwind after a busy day at work. Join them for a sociable *aperitivo* – there's always room for newcomers.

» **Don't leave without** trying a Cardinale cocktail, made with Campari and bitter orange juice. It's one of Rome's oldest drinks and Caffè Tevere makes a mean version.

## CAFFÈ PERÙ

**Map 1; Via di Monserrato 46, Campo de' Fiori; ///below.prepared.only; 06 687 9548**

Hole-in-the wall Caffè Perù lends itself perfectly to an unhurried drink with friends. Since 1933, this unpretentious café has been a favourite meeting place for Romans, offering a warm welcome and affordable drinks (which, let's be honest, can be hard to come by in the heart of a capital city). Nothing beats sipping a beer at one of the bar's tables in the picturesque piazza, surrounded by Baroque palaces and chiming churches.

# Grattachecca Kiosks

***Come summer, there's one drink to beat the heat:* grattachecca. *Once made with snow from the mountains, this 19th-century refreshment sees shaved ice topped with syrups or juice.***

## ALLA FONTE D'ORO

**Map 2; Lungotevere Raffaello Sanzio, Trastevere; ///photo.dollar.sliding; 348 521 0650**

If you visit just one *grattachecca* (pronounced *grat-tah-keh-kkah*) kiosk, it should probably be the city's oldest. Alla Fonte d'Oro has been preparing cooling cups of *grattachecca* since 1913 and it's as pretty as a picture. Sat by the Tiber, the Art Nouveau-style stand is the perfect place to pause for a sweet treat when crossing over from the city centre to Trastevere. And remember: don't drink your *grattachecca* like a cocktail; the locals eat it with a spoon.

## CHIOSCO

**Map 3; Via Giovanni Branca 122, Testaccio; ///friday.haggle.slimy**

Tucked away between Testaccio's market and Roman ruins is Chiosco, a kiosk famed for its *lemoncocco* – the original flavour of *grattachecca*. Made of ice, lemon juice and chunks of coconut, the *lemoncocco* here is also topped with slices of fresh lemon, which the hardy eat (no, really) once they've polished off their *grattachecca*. Don't be turned off if there's a queue at the kiosk – it means you're in the right place.

## IL TEMPIO DELLA GRATTACHECCA

**Map 5; Lungotevere in Augusta, Campo Marzio; ///friday.haggle.slimy**

Yes, this is the most touristy kiosk, with its fridge full of cans of pop and countless posters advertising paninis, but it's too good to miss. Aside from its gorgeous location on the river, the kiosk always has someone hard at work cutting pounds of fruit, so you know your *grattachecca* will be the freshest that money can buy. Once you've ordered, sit at one of the tables and savour your drink.

» **Don't leave without** asking for some fresh watermelon to go with your *grattachecca* – there's nothing better as the sun beats down.

## ER CHIOSCHETTO

**Map 6; Via Magnagrecia 27, San Giovanni; ///gently.sprain.shuttle; 335 656 8978**

Parents have been shepherding their children to this cheerful green-and-yellow kiosk since 1930. Today, charming Felice prepares their refreshments, just as his father and grandfather did before him. His signature *grattachecca* is Dar Chioschetto, a blend of ice, black cherry syrup, tamarind syrup and fresh lemon juice, all topped with black cherries and chunks of coconut.

## Liked by the locals

**"*Grattachecca* isn't just a drink, it's a way of socializing – young and old, families and friends – that has lasted for a century. When Romans slurp it, they feel like they're eating a piece of the city. Come summer, this experience cannot be missed."**

ALESSANDRO SIMONI,
OWNER OF SORA MIRELLA

## SORA MIRELLA

**Map 2; Lungotevere degli Anguillara, Trastevere; ///mixture.piper.pitching**

You know a *grattachecca* kiosk is going to be good when a First Lady of the United States pops by to sample its delights. That's right, Michelle Obama visited Sora Mirella in 2009 and instantly made it the most famous *grattachecca* kiosk in Rome. Aside from wanting to walk in the footsteps of modern-day gods, locals flock here to sample non-traditional flavours, including deliciously boozy concoctions. When the weather is especially hot, groups of friends order alcoholic *grattachecche* before strolling over to Tiber Island, right next to the kiosk, to sunbathe by the river.

## LA SORA MARIA

**Map 5; Via Trionfale 37, Prati; ///recipient.standing.visit**

There's a big reason to love La Sora Maria; it's the women of the Simoni family who have run this *grattachecca* business since 1933. If you're lucky, the 80-something-year-old matriarch Signora Maria will be working the kiosk when you visit, serving your icy drink with stories from the past. The 1970s-style kiosk makes hundreds of *grattachecche* a day during the summer, with thirsty fans forming a (fairly) orderly queue down the street. Aside from the traditional *lemoncocco*, classic flavours include grape and tamarind, which has long been believed to be medicinal.

» **Don't leave without** grabbing a slice of pizza from nearby Bonci's *(p44)*. The pizza at this food-to-go joint is truly legendary thanks to master dough-maker Gabriele Bonci.

# Wine Bars

***How do Romans unwind after a busy day? In the city's welcoming wine bars, naturally. From honest house reds to truly special natural wines, there's a bottle of* vino *for every occasion and taste.***

## ENOTECA L'ANTIDOTO

**Map 2; Vicolo del Bologna 19, Trastevere; ///stress.haven.bonnet; www.enotecalantidoto.com**

Natural wine is having a moment in Rome, and this Trastevere gem is a great spot to swill a glass. The wines here are largely Italian, all organic and biodynamic, plus they change weekly so there's always a new bottle with a different story to sample. Served with the typical warmth of the city, this tempting *enoteca* is just too good to miss.

## PIZZICAROLA

**Map 6; Viale di Villa Pamphili 143, Monteverde; ///daytime.robe.yoga; 068 987 6433**

Some positives were born from the COVID-19 pandemic, like a renewed appreciation for our local neighbourhood stores. And this is why PIZZICaROLA opened in 2022: as a celebratory one-stop shop for all things local. Owner Carola stocks her Monteverde deli with fresh fruit and vegetables that come directly from small farmers. When *aperitivo* hour rolls around, the deli turns into a charming wine bar where Carola will talk you through natural wines and suggest cheese and prosciutto pairings to complement each glass.

## IL GOCCETTO

**Map 1; Via dei Banchi Vecchi 14, Piazza Navona; ///advice.inclined.troubles; 069 944 8583**

Arrive on a Saturday night and you'll spot Il Goccetto's customers before the bar itself. The eclectic crowd of well-dressed Romans (often including a film director or actor) spills out onto the street to mingle among the Vespas – both parked and on the move – while enjoying a glass of the good stuff. Catch the attention of a member of staff among the bustle, and they'll be happy to share their expertise; you'll need it, what with there being 800 wines to choose from.

» **Don't leave without** ordering some creamy buffalo mozzarella and pickled veggies to keep the hunger pangs at bay.

## ENOTECA IL PICCOLO

**Map 1; Via del Governo Vecchio 74, Piazza Navona; ///dramatic.inherit.balanced; 066 880 1746**

Wedged between touristy restaurants touting their wares is this tiny gem – blink and you'll miss it. There's no English menu here, just a smattering of tables and shelf upon shelf lined with bottles of Italian *vino*. Sample one of the traditional ten whites or reds served by the glass before a stroll through nearby Piazza Navona.

# Solo, Pair, Crowd

**A glass of wine and drop of Roman gentility is guaranteed to put you in a good mood.**

## FLYING SOLO

### Wine for one

With both classic and natural wines, RetroVino near Piazza Navona is the place to enjoy a glass with no distractions. Sit at the counter and ask the friendly staff about their most quaffable wines.

## IN A PAIR

### Make a toast for two

Book a table at Pigneto's La Santeria di Mare, the best seafood trattoria in Rome. All-Italian hospitality, simple dishes and the most delicious natural wines are all that's needed to impress your favourite person.

## FOR A CROWD

### A glass in the great outdoors

Outdoor kiosk Fischio, just north of the Vatican, has plenty of outdoor seating and natural wines – perfect for sharing a couple of bottles with your loved ones in the summer months.

## ENOTECA BUCCONE

**Map 5; Via di Ripetta 19/20, Campo Marzio; ///betrayal.spirit.explored; www.enotecabuccone.com**

Once the coach house of a noble family, this welcoming wine shop has been open since the 1960s. Brothers Vincenzo and Francesco (who inherited the shop from their parents) keep a sense of history alive with rustic chandeliers, marble countertops and an antique cash register. Oh, and a treasure trove of traditional wines, of course.

» **Don't leave without** pairing your wine with the *ncapriata* (bean puree with turnip greens) and homemade hummus.

## CIRCOLETTO

**Map 3; Via dei Cerchi 55, Ripa; ///narrow.stuns.dined; 068 377 7691**

You don't go to hipster hotspot Circoletto by mistake – you go with a purpose. And that purpose is to swig natural Italian wines and scoff pastrami pizza. Chat to the locals at the long, sociable tables indoors or take your goodies outdoors and relish the views of the ancient chariot-racing stadium the Circus Maximus.

## IL VINAIETTO

**Map 1; Via del Monte della Farina 38, Campo de' Fiori; ///popped.edges.diamonds; 066 880 6989**

This classic spot hasn't changed since the 1960s. It's got the same black-and-white chequered tiles, left-wing posters and no Wi-Fi. Il Vinaietto is all about excellent wine and excellent conversation, which is largely enjoyed standing on the street outside.

# Craft Beer Spots

***Artisanal beer has been a thing in Rome for over 20 years, with independent brew pubs scattered across the city. These craft beer spots are distinctly Roman: no frills, no hipsters and not in the least bit snobbish.***

## TREEFOLK'S PUBLIC HOUSE

**Map 3; Viale di Trastevere 192, Trastevere; ///cross.glove.printers; www.treefolkspublichouse.com**

Dark wooden panelling, leather chesterfields and richly patterned rugs: Treefolk's has all the vibes of a traditional British pub. The theme continues at the bar, where chocolatey stouts and bitter ales from small brewers in Blighty dominate the taps. Looking for something lighter? Thankfully there are a handful of refreshing Italian IPAs and Czech Pilsners, too.

## PORK'N'ROLL

**Map 6; Via Carlo Caneva 15, Tiburtino; ///cuts.gathers.paths; www.porknroll.com**

This joint may be out in suburbia but it remains a favourite thanks to its magical rule of three: beer, cured meats and live music. Owner Gerardo keeps locals returning with his hand-picked selection of IPAs

Arrive at Pork'n'Roll around 7pm – that's when you'll find a rock band setting up for the night.

from Italian microbreweries and prosciutto, lovingly handmade by him and his brother (it takes a lot of time and experience to make prosciutto, don't you know).

## ARTISAN

**Map 6; Via degli Aurunci 7, San Lorenzo; ///showdown.obstruction.beeline; 06 9357 1339**

Beer experts Emanuele and Giuseppe have perfected this welcoming taproom, offering a weekly rotation of international brews and friendly advice to help find the right beer for you. A *vino* drinker in your party? Want to end your night with a whiskey? Artisanal spirits and wines are also on hand, so everyone's happy.

» **Don't leave without** trying one of the Scandinavian beers. Emanuele and Giuseppe love them and can make recommendations.

## MA CHE SIETE VENUTI A FÀ

**Map 2; Via Benedetta 25, Trastevere; ///lifelong.demoted.instead; www.football-pub.com**

Where better to wet your whistle than at Rome's very first craft beer pub? Since 2001, this dark little taproom has been pulling pints of Italian, European and US beers for thirsty beer enthusiasts and football fanatics, who come to watch the match on the bar's big screen. You might even hear the pub's name being chanted; *ma cha siete venuti a fà* means "what did you come here for?" and is a mocking taunt sung by fans of Rome's Lazio football team.

## Liked by the locals

**"Many visitors don't realize that Rome loves craft beer more than any other Italian city. The first true Italian craft breweries were born here and in the surrounding area, and all of us publicans love to make known these refreshing flavours of the area."**

FEDERICO FELIZIANI,
OWNER OF PIZZERIA L'ELEMENTARE

## PIZZERIA L'ELEMENTARE

**Map 2; Via Benedetta 23, Trastevere; ///skins.allergy.older; www.pizzerialelementare.it**

Pizza just hits better with craft beer. Well, so say pizza chef Mirko Rizzo and beer expert Federico Feliziani, who gifted the good people of Trastevere l'Elementare. The pizzeria plates up perfectly baked, perfectly crispy Roman pizzas alongside a tempting range of national craft brews. Our favourite pairing? Probably the pizza *puttanesca*, loaded with burrata, olives and anchovies, and a pint of IPA from Lazio's Eastside Brewing Company.

**» Don't leave without ordering something from the *fritti* (fried) menu. The mouth-wateringly good lasagne *supplì* are made of fried cubes of lasagne filled with beef ragu and a bechamel sauce.**

## OPEN BALADIN

**Map 1; Via degli Specchi 6, Jewish Quarter; ///trim.prelude.budget; www.baladin.it/open-baladin-roma**

Baladin's story begins in Piedmont, in northern Italy. Owner Teo Musso grew up in a farming family and never liked the taste of his dad's homemade wine, much preferring beer. He was so fond of it, in fact, that in 1986 he opened a dedicated beer pub, stocking 200 labels across Europe. But he wanted more. In the late 1990s, he travelled to Belgium to master the craft of beer-making. Upon returning to Piedmont, Teo started brewing his own craft beer in old milk vats, in the pub's garage. And so Italy's most loved craft beer was born. Yes, you'll see Baladin bottles in Rome's supermarkets, but you'll really discover what the fuss is about at the brand's pub.

# An evening of **wine tasting**

In Italy, wine isn't a luxury, it's a way of life. Even in the days of the Roman Empire, everyone in high society was sipping *vino*. It all started with the Etruscans, who brought winemaking to the Italian peninsula. Fast forward to today and Italy is one of the top wine producers worldwide. From rich and bold reds in Puglia and Piedmont to sparkling whites in Veneto and Lombardy, the country has a wine for every palate. And, starting from lunchtime, it's always wine o'clock. Cheers to that!

**1. Il Vinaietto**
Via del Monte della Farina 38, Campo de' Fiori; 06 6880 6989
///chills.cooking.dusty

**2. Angolo Divino**
Via dei Balestrari 12–14, Campo de' Fiori; www.angolodivino.it
///splint.crowned.swam

**3. Vineyarts**
Corso Vittorio Emanuele II 154, Campo de' Fiori; www.vineyarts.com
///cases.rainfall.boring

**4. Rimessa Roscioli**
Via del Conservatorio 58, Campo de' Fiori; www.rimessaroscioli.com
///boxer.obeyed.fancy

**Pancrazio dal 1922**
*///risky.dabbled.tingled*

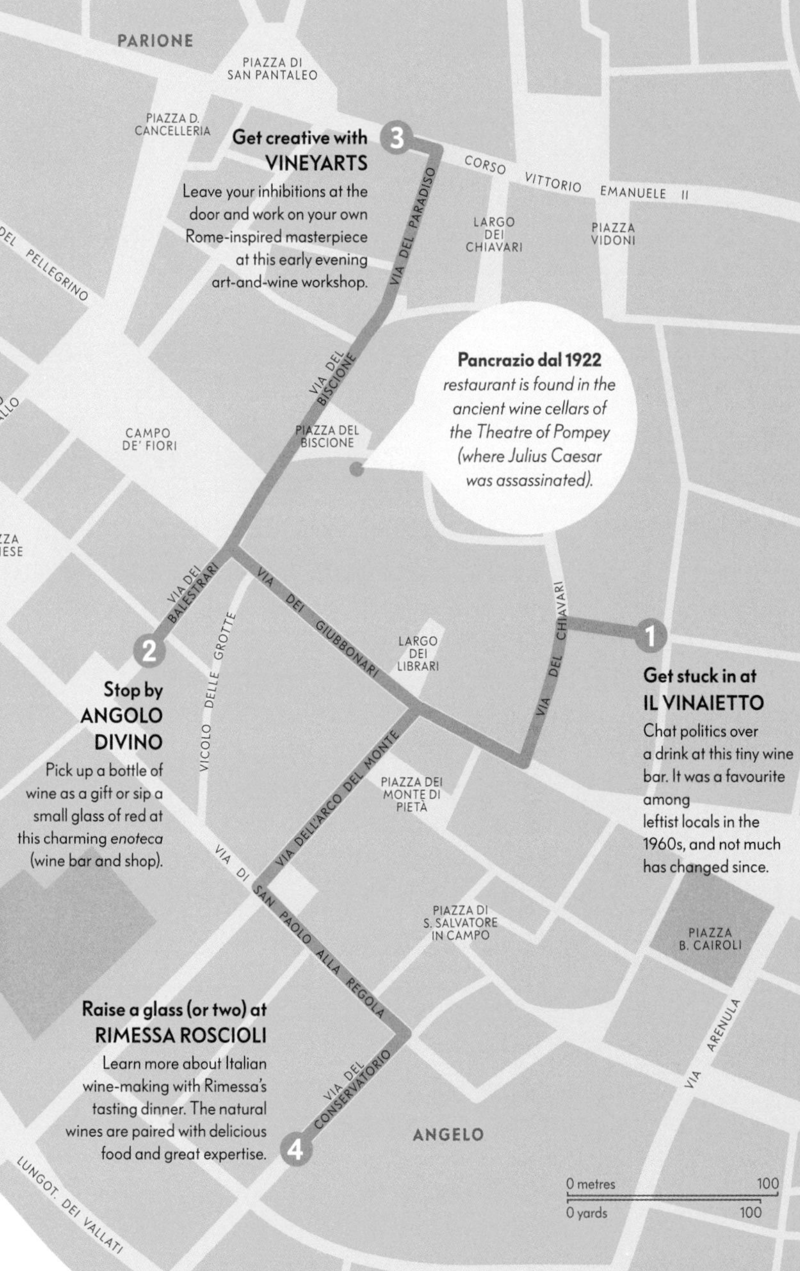
PARIONE
PIAZZA DI SAN PANTALEO
PIAZZA D. CANCELLERIA
3
Get creative with
VINEYARTS
Leave your inhibitions at the door and work on your own Rome-inspired masterpiece at this early evening art-and-wine workshop.
VIA DEL PARADISO
CORSO VITTORIO EMANUELE II
LARGO DEI CHIAVARI
PIAZZA VIDONI
DEL PELLEGRINO
VIA DEL BISCIONE
Pancrazio dal 1922
restaurant is found in the ancient wine cellars of the Theatre of Pompey (where Julius Caesar was assassinated).
CAMPO DE' FIORI
PIAZZA DEL BISCIONE
VIA DEI BALESTRARI
VIA DEI GIUBBONARI
VICOLO DELLE GROTTE
LARGO DEI LIBRARI
VIA DEL CHIAVARI
1
Get stuck in at
IL VINAIETTO
Chat politics over a drink at this tiny wine bar. It was a favourite among leftist locals in the 1960s, and not much has changed since.
2
Stop by
ANGOLO DIVINO
Pick up a bottle of wine as a gift or sip a small glass of red at this charming *enoteca* (wine bar and shop).
VIA DELL'ARCO DEL MONTE
PIAZZA DEI MONTE DI PIETÀ
VIA DI SAN PAOLO ALLA REGOLA
PIAZZA DI S. SALVATORE IN CAMPO
PIAZZA B. CAIROLI
VIA ARENULA
Raise a glass (or two) at
RIMESSA ROSCIOLI
Learn more about Italian wine-making with Rimessa's tasting dinner. The natural wines are paired with delicious food and great expertise.
VIA DEL CONSERVATORIO
4
ANGELO
LUNGOT. DEI VALLATI
0 metres 100
0 yards 100

# SHOP

*Made-to-measure hats and suits, timeless vintage fashion, epic reads and delicious treats: when it comes to shopping, there's no place like Rome.*

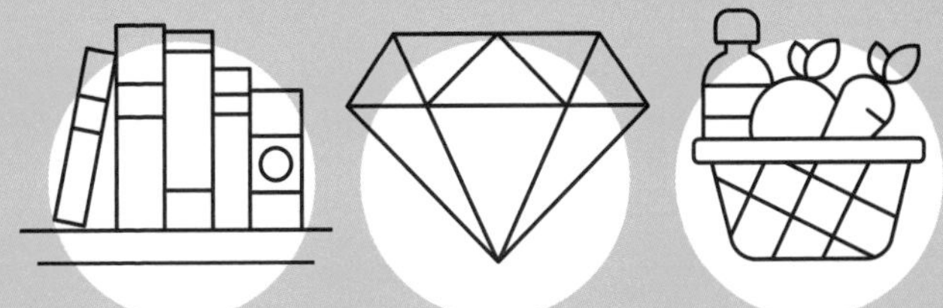

# Beloved Markets

***It's in local markets that Romans get stuff done: catching up on all the news with their neighbours, picking up food for dinner and finding fresh looks for the season ahead.***

## MERCATO VIA SANNIO

**Map 6; Via Sannio, San Giovanni; ///workers.massing.crown; 328 858 9811**

Under the looming shadow of the Basilica of San Giovanni (which, surprisingly, is Rome's principal church, not St Peter's Basilica in the Vatican), treasure seekers hunt for quirky bargains. Piles of military surplus, vintage fur coats, pre-loved sportswear and fishing gear are both varied and well priced; it's no wonder that actors and costume designers are often spotted looking for inspiration here.

## MERCATO DI TESTACCIO

**Map 3; Via Aldo Manuzio 66b, Testaccio; ///definite.powerful.junior; www.mercatoditestaccio.it**

Make like the Testaccio locals (*Testaccini* to Romans) and swing by this neighbourhood market first thing, before the rest of Rome arrives. The market specializes in fish, meat, fruit and veg, and the stall owners have plenty of tips on the best ways to cook your

On a budget? Fish is often affordable here. Try the anchovies: they're both cheap and full of flavour.

produce. Stick around for lunch: the market's gastronomic food stalls are famous, serving perfectly prepared pizza and paninis.

## BORGHETTO FLAMINIO

**Map 5; Piazza della Marina 32, Flaminio; ///hampers.values.free; 06 588 0517**

If you fantasize about finding pre-loved Prada or second-hand Chanel when scouring the rails, then Sunday's Borghetto Flaminio is the market for you. Small in size but big on labels, the market is a much calmer and more civilized affair than your typical flea market rummage, with organized stalls of curated clothing, jewellery and accessories. Yes, there is a small entrance fee, but the actual product prices are pretty reasonable considering what's on offer.

## MERCATO DI CAMPO DE' FIORI

**Map 1; Campo de' Fiori; ///hardly.pits.canyons**

You wouldn't know that Caravaggio killed a man in this square (apparently over a game of tennis), nor that grisly executions took place here in the 16th and 17th centuries. Today Campo de' Fiori is a sociable spot. The piazza trills with friendly chatter as locals peruse the city's most popular fruit and veg market (even Rome's top chefs are regulars), open every Monday through Saturday.

» **Don't leave without** seeking out Franca, a die-hard Roma football fan who has been serving customers at lightning speed for 70 years.

# Solo, Pair, Crowd

**Prefer to peruse a market on your own? Making plans with your posse? Rome has a market for every occasion.**

## FLYING SOLO

### Show your walls some love

Day to yourself? Make a beeline for Mercato Antiquario Piazza Borghese, a cute market selling antique prints, maps and postcards. Find a few pieces for your home before heading to Il Marchese *(p141)* for a drink.

## IN A PAIR

### Wine and dine as a pair

Take your other half to Mercato Trionfale, a covered market in Prati. Here there are 200 stalls dedicated to all things food and drink so you can spend an entire afternoon snacking and sipping.

## FOR A CROWD

### Low-key bites with your besties

Planning lunch with the gang? Campagna Amica is a sustainable farmers' market not far from the Colosseum. Gorge on stuffed paninis and arancini before walking it off around the Roman Forum.

## MERCATO ESQUILINO

**Map 4; Via Principe Amedeo 184, Esquilino; ///apply.stump.croak; 329 213 0617**

Standing firm against gentrification, Mercato Esquilino perfectly captures the welcoming charm and cultural diversity that has long existed in Rome. Chinese grocers, Roman fishmongers, halal butchers – everyone coexists happily at this down-to-earth market.

## PORTA PORTESE

**Map 2; Piazza di Porta Portese, Trastevere; ///writings.burying.zips; www.portaportesemarket.it**

Every Sunday morning, the roads around the ancient gate of Porta Portese are closed to make way for hundreds of savvy peddlers, each piling their stalls high with... *stuff*. Antique furniture, glassware, jewellery, books and vinyl all spill from their tables onto the pavement. It's impossible to leave this treasure trove of a flea market empty-handed.

## CITTÀ ECOSOLIDALE

**Map 3; Via del Porto Fluviale 2, Ostiense; ///regard.riots.remodels; 06 5730 0510**

Romans are very attached to this market, which is a hodgepodge of second-hand clothing, furniture, kitchenware, books and toys. Run by volunteers – including former drug addicts – the market's proceeds go toward charities both near and far.

» **Don't leave without** giving an extra donation. The market helps feed the homeless here in Rome and all contributions are warmly received.

# Classic Style

***Milan may be Italy's fashion capital but Rome is a stronghold of traditional tailoring and craftsmanship. Whether you're after a bespoke suit, new tie or chic hat, these Roman stalwarts will make you feel truly dandy.***

## LA CRAVATTA SU MISURA

**Map 1; Via Metastasio 17, Campo Marzio; ///general.after.tribal; www.cravattasumisura.it**

A tie reflects the wearer's taste and character – so says *cravattificio* (tie shop) owner Melania Flamini, anyway. With over 30 years of experience, Melania carefully crafts ties to order, adding embroidered initials, logos and other personal touches. Whether you're after a bow tie, cravat or *foulard* (square silk scarf), she'll custom make you the perfect item to set off your *Roman Holiday* aesthetic.

## GAMMARELLI SARTORIA

**Map 1; Via di Santa Chiara 34, Piazza Navona; ///crafted.rested.remake; www.gammarelli.com**

It's not every day that you meet the Pope's official tailor. Tucked behind the Pantheon, this historic shop specializes in ecclesiastical clothing. It all started in 1798, when Giovanni Antonio Gammarelli became the official master tailor to the Roman clergy. Since then, the privilege of dressing thousands of priests and hundreds of bishops, cardinals and popes has been passed down through six generations of Gammarellis, with Lorenzo Gammarelli the present tailor. (Fun fact: during conclave, when cardinals meet to decide who should be the next head of the Catholic church, Gammarelli makes not one but three sets of robes. Why? Because it's not known whether the new pope will be small, medium or large in build.) Exquisite handmade cassocks and vestments are on display inside the shop, as are a range of affordable handmade Italian socks – the ideal sartorial souvenir.

**» Don't leave without walking two minutes down the road to Antica Cartotecnica, a charming pen shop that was founded in 1930.**

## FENDI

**Map 5; Largo Goldoni 420, Campo Marzio; ///runners.glitter.haggis; www.fendi.com**

We can't not mention fashion house Fendi. In 1918, Adele Casagrande opened a leather and fur shop on Via del Plebiscito, renaming the store Fendi when she married Edoardo Fendi a few years later. The couple's five daughters took over the business in 1947; Paola, Franca, Carla, Alda and Anna were known as the *cinque sorelle Fendi* (the five Fendi sisters). But it wasn't until 1965, when the sisters hired Karl Lagerfeld as creative director, that Fendi was firmly cemented as a hallmark of classic Italian style. Pay homage to this dynasty of fashion giants by visiting the label's elegant flagship store, set in a luxurious 17th-century palazzo. Alternatively, just gaze longingly at the stylishly dressed mannequins in the windows.

## ANTICA MANIFATTURA CAPPELLI

**Map 5; Via degli Scipioni 46, Prati; ///january.luggage.recital; 063 972 5679**

A family of Tuscan hatmakers opened this lovely shop in the 1930s and ran the business for three generations until Mr Loris Cirri fell ill in 2003. Thankfully, designer Patrizia Fabri – a regular at the shop – bought the business, retaining the 2,000 wooden hat forms displayed inside. Since then, the shop's fetching creations have appeared on runways, movie sets and, of course, on Rome's fashionable streets.

## SARTORIA RIPENSE

**Map 5; Via di Ripetta 38; Campo Marzio; ///native.mediate.rail; www.sartoriaripense.ecwid.com**

New kid on the block Ripense might've opened in 2000 but the shop is wholly traditional in thinking. Tailor Andrea learned his craft from his skilled *nonno* (grandfather), and opened the store as a celebration of classic Italian style (think chic suits and tasselled loafers).

## ANTONIO AGLIETTI SHOEMAKER

**Map 3; Via Giovanni Branca 47, Testaccio; ///assure.cutback.fruit; 06 5730 0399**

Upon entering this old-school *bottega* (workshop), you'll be greeted by shoemaker Antonio – and the heady scent of Italian leather. Antonio will soon be on the floor, showing you swatches and tracing your feet for a truly unique pair of made-to-measure shoes.

» **Don't leave without** asking Antonio to monogram your initials onto the soles for a personal touch.

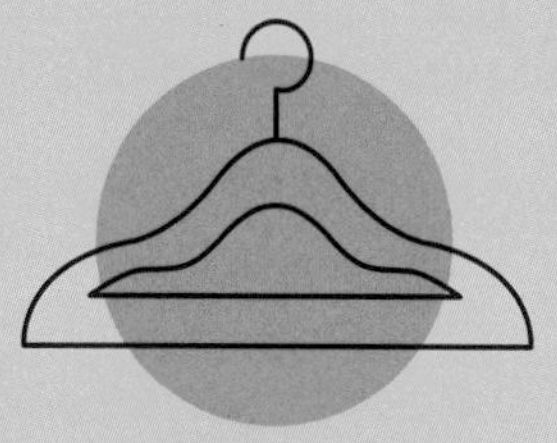

## Liked by the locals

**"Rome is the cradle of great Made in Italy tailoring, and the city embodies all the uniqueness of Italian talent and style. Here you can find tailors of yesteryear, such as Sartoria Ripense, which makes strictly bespoke suits for men."**

ANTONIO AMENDOLA,
FOUNDER OF *ROMEING* MAGAZINE

# Chic Accessories

***Romans know that it just takes a statement necklace, pair of stylish sunglasses or hand-crafted bag to elevate an outfit. So make like a local and ignore high street chains – hit the city's artisan boutiques instead.***

## MONDELLO OTTICA

**Map 6; Via Gregorio VII 320–322, Regola; ///agreed.remarked.faster; www.otticamondello.it**

For Italians, an outfit isn't complete without a pair of stylish sunnies, and where better to get some than family-run Mondello Ottica? A photography shop in the 1960s, the place evolved into an eyewear store in the 1980s. Today it stocks both high-end brands like Balenciaga and lesser-known labels, such as Los Angeles designer Jacques Marie Mage and Japanese brand Factory900.

## CO.RO. JEWELS

**Map 1; Via della Scrofa 52, Piazza Navona; ///audible.earl.fresh; www.corojewels.com**

The perfect souvenir? You can't go wrong with a piece of handcrafted jewellery inspired by Rome's most historic sights. Architects Costanza and Giulia take inspiration from buildings around the world – including their home town – when making silver- and gold-plated jewellery. Elegant rings include detail from the domed roof of the Pantheon and cuff bracelets reflect the arched aqueduct on the Appian Way. Pieces range from €50 to €600, so there's something for every budget.

## ANNA RETICO DESIGN

**Map 2; Vicolo del Cinque 13, Trastevere; ///same.star.section; www.annareticodesign.it**

Necklaces strung with tiny toy cars, earrings made from crocheted PVC, rings and cufflinks crafted from used glass: Anna Retico's whimsical jewellery is both original and sustainable. Have a specific request? Anna can also craft something from recycled metal, scrap plastic and fused glass just for you.

## HANG ROMA

**Map 4; Via degli Zingari 32, Monti; ///pitchers.rates.pebble; www.hangroma.it**

What do all Italians have in common? A beautiful leather bag, that's what. And for locals, Hang Roma is a safe bet for a quality shoulder bag, backpack or shopper. Founders Federica and Valentina met at Rome's Academy of Industrial Design and decided to join forces, opening a boutique that honours the centuries-old craft of leatherwork. Made from vegetable-tanned leather from Tuscany, these beautiful bags are sure to last a lifetime.

» **Don't leave without** checking out the Ripa bag. The shoulder bag doubles as a rucksack and can be customized with bespoke stitching.

## FARAONI

**Map 1; Via Banchi Vecchi 137, Campo de' Fiori; ///response.booth.compound; 06 683 2832**

Mosaics date back to ancient times but micromosaics were a thing of the 18th and 19th centuries, when Europeans traipsed around Italy on the Grand Tour. Teeny tiny pieces of glass were arranged into images and scenes on pendants and brooches here in Rome, which travellers could easily transport home as a souvenir. Today Luigi Faraoni and Silvia Grieco keep the craft alive.

## ATELIER MARLOES MANDAAT

**Map 4; Via Urbana 136, Monti; ///staples.motion.mammals; www.marloesmandaat.com**

Dutch-born designer Marloes Mandaat spent two decades working as a stylist for big fashion houses like Gucci, Armani and Chanel before starting her own brand. In her small Roman atelier, she designs timeless soft-leather handbags and simple, classy jewellery – all the

### Try it!
### MAKE A MICROMOSAIC

Want to try your hand at the ancient art of micromosaics? Studio Cassio runs various classes, including a jewellery workshop where you'll fill a necklace pendant with a micromosaic *(www.studiocassio.com)*.

chic accessories needed for a modern Italian look. Even better, Marloes uses exclusively Italian materials and works with local production companies in and around Rome to craft her designs.

## ANDREANO

**Map 1; Piazza di Tor Sanguigna 3, Piazza Navona; ///pilots.halt.outdone; www.andreanoshop.com**

When Rome is gripped by a particularly cold winter, locals descend upon glove shop Andreano, rubbing their hands expectantly. This chocolate box of a shop stocks every type of glove imaginable: leather, suede, crocheted, fleece-lined, cashmere-lined, fur-trimmed. The genial staff advise on the best shape and materials for the wearer, offering glove after glove until customers find the perfect pair.

## ESSENZIALMENTE LAURA

**Map 1; Via dei Coronari 57, Ponte; ///loves.compiled.fishery; www.essenzialmentelaura.it**

A spritz of perfume really does complete an ensemble, doesn't it? Having created colognes and candles for the likes of the Vatican, Laura Bosetti Tonatto is Italy's most famous nose; a bottle of her gorgeous scent can be found in many an Italian handbag. A collection of 62 affordable perfumes await in Laura's charming apothecary-style shop – there's even a spicy *Incenso delle Chiese di Roma*, which will transport you to any one of the city's 900 incense-heavy churches.

» **Don't leave without** perusing Laura's collection of shower gels, body lotions and oils – ideal for someone who needs pampering (aka you).

# Vintage Gems

***There are two types of vintage shops in Rome: old-school spots that specialize in classic fashion and new-school shops that are all about modern vintage. If one thing unites them, it's a love for style.***

## SITENNE

**Map 4; Via Cairoli 55, Esquilino; ///letters.fail.padlock; www.sitenne.com**

Shop manager Alberta likes to think of SiTenne as more of a dressing room than a vintage shop – she does have a background in theatre costume design, after all. Her loyal clientele of photographers, film directors and stage actors take advantage of her rental and tailoring services, trying on 1960s mini-dresses and borrowing mid-century suits for upcoming shoots. Not in showbiz? No fear, Alberta will still welcome you with open arms (and a tape measure).

## VO.RE.CO.

**Map 2; Via della Lungara 141a, Trastevere; ///nutrients.oaks.airless; www.voreco.it**

Tucked away in a corner of Trastevere, opposite the city's historical prison, you'll find a tiny vintage shop run by volunteers and prisoners at the end of their sentence. It's as much about reintegrating prisoners back into society as it is selling second-hand wears. The folks of Trastevere love donating to this store, handing over pre-loved Prada and timeless pearl necklaces, which are all sold on for a snip. Note that it's cash only, and there is a serious lack of ATMs nearby, so take out some euros in advance.

**» Don't leave without swinging by Villa Farnesina – one of the most gorgeous palaces (and gardens) in all of Rome.**

## KING SIZE

**Map 4; Via Leonina 78, Monti; ///willing.dressy.happier; 340 076 6683**

Children of the 1980s and 90s: we see you. Nostalgic for the brightly coloured shell suits of your youth? Time to revisit a pair of denim dungarees? King Size won't let you down – even the killer soundtrack will transport you back to the good old days.

## ITALO DAL 1968

**Map 1; Via del Pellegrino 122, Campo de' Fiori; ///ranches.starch.just; 338 992 3520**

After World War II, Mr Italo set out to inject a little sartorial style and joy back into the wardrobes of ordinary Romans. His second-hand clothing shop, packed to the brim with quality wool coats and smart linen jackets, quickly became a destination and caught the attention of movie-makers – just about every film shot in Rome during *La Dolce Vita* years includes pieces from Mr Italo. Today his son happily continues his legacy.

## HUMANA VINTAGE

**Map 4; Via Leonina 38, Monti; ///edge.active.decency; www.humanavintage.it**

Like to know your money is doing good in the world? Charity shop Humana Vintage is the one for you. Supporting good causes both in Italy and abroad, the Monti outpost stocks pieces of a lifetime at incredible prices. Spending €5 on a Valentino skirt isn't unheard of.

## OMERO E CECILIA

**Map 1; Via del Governo Vecchio 110, Piazza Navona; ///extremes.flipper.relax; 06 683 3506**

Vintage shops line Via del Governo Vecchio so, to find this gem, pay attention to the building number – or look for a short, grey-haired lady. This is Cecilia who, with her partner Omero, has been selling vintage clothing for 40 years. Okay, the prices are a little higher than elsewhere but the quality is undisputed: Gucci bags from the 1970s, hand-sewn lace veils, barely worn cashmere jumpers.

**» Don't leave without** asking about Celia's celebrity customers. Diane Keaton, Keanu Reeves and Alessandro Michele have all shopped here.

## PIFEBO

**Map 4; Via dei Serpenti 135, Monti; ///fronted.quiz.topped; www.pifebo.com**

It might be in white-collar Monti but this branch of Pifebo is all about modern vintage fashion. On weekends, the store swarms with teens and students, all on the hunt for Kappa sweatshirts, pairs of pre-loved Levi's and pastel-coloured Ralph Lauren shirts from the 1980s.

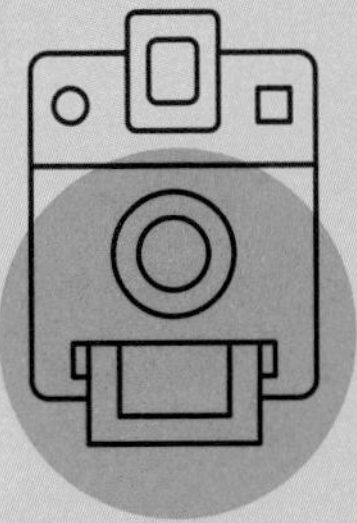

## Liked by the locals

**"In a world that expects us to keep up with the latest trends, it's fun to embrace the past by wearing vintage. That's exactly what vintage-lovers in Rome think. And Romans also know that Monti is the vintage hub of the city... and Pifebo is its king!"**

ANGELICA BONACCHI, ENGINEERING STUDENT AT UNIVERSITY OF TOR VERGATA

# Book Nooks

***Stories are woven into every plinth and pillar in Rome, and locals are very proud of the fact. And when they're not regaling tales of myths and legends, they're recommending a read from their local bookshop.***

## OTHERWISE

**Map 1; Via del Governo Vecchio 80, Piazza Navona; ///various.cloth.lame; 06 687 9825**

Locals and expats were over the moon when this independent English-language bookshop opened in 2017. Up-to-the-minute books by British, Australian and North American writers line the store's curated shelves, along with delightful handwritten recommends and reviews by staff. That's not all: Otherwise also hosts live readings, author events and book clubs. It's as much of a community centre as it is a bookshop.

## ALTROQUANDO

**Map 1; Via del Governo Vecchio 82, Piazza Navona; ///trunk.relaxing.nasal; www.altroquando.com**

Across the street from Otherwise sits its older sister, Altroquando. Specializing chiefly in Italian non-fiction, the store's eclectic offerings include travel, cookery and photography tomes, though it's the fabulous collection of movie posters and books on cinema that get locals hot under the collar. That, and the bookshop's basement pub – the perfect spot to flick through Fellini's biography with a pint.

## BOOKTIQUE

**Map 1; Via della Stelletta 17, Campo Marzio; ///concerts.rankings.liked; www.booktique.info**

Romans Daniele, Fabio and Filippo had a vision: a boutique-style bookshop where beautiful and inspiring books in Italian and English sit beside stylish items for the home (think art prints, candles and coffee cups). The result was Booktique, a modern bookshop and concept store rolled into one. You'll enter looking for a stylish book for your coffee table and leave with presents for all your loved ones back home.

**» Don't leave without** one of Booktique's tote bags, which have typical Roman sayings splashed across them. We like the tote with *Ahó* – the local way of saying "hello", but also "watch out" or "what the hell?"

## GIUFÀ LIBRERIA CAFFÈ

**Map 6; Via degli Aurunci, San Lorenzo; ///caravan.harder.mouse; www.libreriagiufa.it**

Vaulted cellar ceilings and chequered flooring make for a rather charming setting at this cute San Lorenzo bookshop. Pop in to peruse the shelves of graphic novels, comics and children's books, or the collection of Italian-language fiction from Italy's small publishing houses. As the name suggests, there's also a café – ideal for soaking up the ambience with an espresso.

## OPEN DOOR BOOKSHOP

**Map 2; Via della Lungaretta 23, Trastevere; ///leap.supposed.answers; www.opendoorbookshop.it**

Unsurprisingly, there's an open door policy at Open Door Bookshop. The second-hand store is run by sisters Lavinia, Paola and Sabina, who treat everyone who enters like family. Looking to brush up on your Italian? They'll teach you some words while passing you provocative Italian literature. After a Penguin classic? Dusty crates will be rifled through until an Orwell or Austen is found. No plans for later? They'll insist you return for the shop's evening jazz performance.

## ALMOST CORNER SHOP

**Map 2; Via del Moro 45, Trastevere; ///flanks.sailing.observe; 06 583 6942**

It might be an English-language bookshop but every type of Roman can be seen at this local institution, headed up by bookworm Dermot O'Connell. Here, students shop for the term's reading list, local workers look for something titillating to read in their lunch hour and long-timers flick through history tomes. If they're lucky, Dermot might be passing through to check on his staff and stock, and will dish out suggestions.

## FRAB'S AT CONTEMPORARY CLUSTER

**Map 4; Via Merulana 248, Esquilino; ///drops.awards.stuns; www.frabsmagazines.com**

Tucked away in a 19th-century palazzo (where various scenes for *Roman Holiday* were filmed), Contemporary Cluster is a modern art gallery with a bookshop like no other. Vintage floor-to-ceiling wooden cabinets that once occupied Rome's Museum of Oriental Art today display cool, collectible indie magazines. It's a great place to spend an hour on a rainy afternoon, sat in one of the velvet armchairs flicking through publications on art, music, wine, feminism and sustainability.

**» Don't leave without** **checking out Contemporary Cluster's changing art and design exhibitions for an extra dose of culture.**

## LIBRERIA TRASTEVERE

**Map 2; Via della Lungaretta 90e, Trastevere; ///flushes.remotes.informal; 06 589 4710**

Bookshops don't come more charming than this one. Once a mini publishing house, now a fully fledged bookshop, Libreria is a shrine to the lesser-known heroes of the literary world. The welcoming shop champions books from smaller publishing houses, including philosophy, travel and children's titles, as well as fiction (in Italian and English). And, when it comes to bookish tips, the *librai* (booksellers) really know their stuff – they never miss a beat. No wonder Libreria is a favourite with Romans buying books for their growing "to read" pile.

### Try it!
### BOOKCROSSING

At café kiosk and library Bibliobar *(Lungotevere Castello)*, locals enjoy bookcrossing. You take a book and leave one you've read in its place, then order a coffee and enjoy at one of the kiosk's tables.

# Gourmet Treats

***It goes without saying: Rome is a foodie city. Locals are forever popping into their local deli (or* pizzicarolo*) to stock up on cheese, ham, wine and pasta – all the trimmings needed to make a feast for their family.***

## SALUMERIA VOLPETTI

**Map 3; Via Marmorata 47, Testaccio; ///arena.paving.tests; www.volpetti.com**

Dozens of dried hams hang above the meat counter at this popular Testaccio deli, which has been keeping the locals' cupboards well stocked since 1973. It's not all cured meats, mind; the *pizzicarolo* bursts at the seams with gourmet cheeses, tempting tins of pâté, top-quality oils, jars of juicy olives and beautifully packaged pastas – we're talking the kind of packaging that's too pretty to rip.

## LA TRADIZIONE

**Map 5; Via Cipro 8e, Prati; ///nasal.gushes.public; www.latradizione.it**

*Nonne* are regulars at this old-world *pizzicarolo*, loading their baskets with cured meats and wedges of cheese before ordering a panini for lunch. Set up by two Umbrians in the 1980s, La Tradizione is all about – you guessed it – traditional products from across the country. Totally overwhelmed by its offerings? You can't go wrong with a hunk of the *coglioni di mulo*, a speciality salami from Abruzzo.

## TRIMANI ENOTECA

**Map 4; Via Goito 20, Termini; ///marshes.steps.rates; 06 446 9661**

When it comes to shopping for wine, Rome's oldest wine shop is a safe bet. Trimani has been run by the same family since 1821 and they really know a Barolo from a Barbera. Specializing in Italian wine, the *enoteca* stocks more than 5,000 bottles, so you're guaranteed to find a good vintage to slosh into your weekend ragu.

» **Don't leave without** booking a wine tasting here – perfect for selecting a couple of bottles for your next dinner party.

## BISCOTTIFICIO INNOCENTI

**Map 2; Via della Luce 21, Trastevere; ///area.backward.helpful; 06 580 3926**

When a friend is celebrating a birthday, Romans traditionally gift biscotti and, nine times out of ten, they're from this cute spot. Stefania is the third generation to run the city's last remaining small-batch baked-goods shop, firing up the same oven that her predecessors used in the 1960s. She lovingly makes every sweet treat by hand: every imaginable flavour of *biscotto*, plus chocolate nougat, panettone, and even off-cuts of bakes that don't go to plan (called "wrong biscuits"). This is the place to buy a treat for a friend, birthday or not, and enjoy some chitchat with Stefania, one of the loveliest ladies in all of Rome.

## ERCOLI 1928

**Map 5; Via Montello 26, Prati; ///porch.early.pillows; www.ercoli1928.com**

Long before New York had Eataly, Rome had Ercoli. First opened in 1928, the food hall is both a place to stock up on quality meats, cheese, oils and vinegars as well as a lovely spot to meet friends for an *aperitivo*. There are a couple of branches across the city, like in genteel Parioli and ultra-cool Trastevere, but the original Prati outpost is the most iconic.

## TARTUFI DAL BOSCO

**Map 4; Via del Gambero 13, Campo Marzio; ///iceberg.goes.roving; www.tartufidalbosco.it**

Surely there's nothing more gourmet than the rarest of Italian treasures: the truffle. This emporium of *tartufa*-related products is *the* shop to treat yourself to a bottle of truffle oil, ready-made truffle sauce or some fresh truffles, providing they're in season (generally late autumn into early spring). After settling up, celebrate your purchases with a glass of wine and some truffle-inspired nibbles at the shop's deli counter.

## DROGHERIA INNOCENZI

**Map 2; Via Natale del Grande 31, Trastevere; ///puzzled.major.nearly; 06 581 2725**

Welcome to the grocery shop of your dreams: packets of dried pasta teetering on shelves, biscuit boxes arranged in towering stacks, huge sacks of dried spices and beans, and so much more besides. The old-school *drogheria* (grocer) has been run by the Innocenzi family since

Looking to buy some dried pasta? Rummo is a trusted, quality brand and widely available.

1932. And yes, all the Italian favourites are here, but this place has lots of international offerings too, so you'll find some tempting treats from home and abroad.

## PANELLA

**Map 4; Via Merulana 54, Monti; ///targeted.kicks.liked; www.panellaroma.com**

Picking up a loaf of bread at Panella is never a quick errand. With a century of experience, the bakery makes 70 different types of mouth-watering bread. You'll spend 15 minutes deciding whether to choose a seeded rye bread or country loaf, Sardinian *coccoi* or Ferrarese cross. Once you've finally chosen, the staff will ask if you'd also like an espresso, or a chocolate-stuffed *sfogliatella* (crispy pastry). You won't be able to resist, trust us.

## ANTICA CACIARA

**Map 2; Via San Francesco a Ripa, 140 a/b, Trastevere; ///gadget.forum.puppets; 06 581 2815**

Want to master the art of making *cacio e pepe*? First things first: you'll need a quality pecorino for this classic Roman dish. Cheesemonger Roberto has been working behind the counter here since 1966 (though the cheese shop itself dates back to 1900), and will serve you with both a smile and expert advice on which pecorino the dish requires.

» **Don't leave without** continuing on to Trastevere's Ercoli 1928 to pick up some pasta and pepper to complete your *cacio e pepe*.

**Grab a treat from**
**BISCOTTIFICIO ARTIGIANO INNOCENTI**

Follow the warm scent of butter to find some serious biscotti at this family-run bakery, which still uses a vintage oven.

**Top off your look at**
**ANTICA CAPPELLERIA MARI**

Venture into this classic hat shop, first opened in 1921. You'll find lots of famous styles – even Stetsons.

**Lose track of time at**
**POLVERE DI TEMPO**

Admire the intricate details of Adrian Rodriguez Cozzani's handmade clocks, hourglasses and sundials. The shop name means "dust of time", a nod to its time-keeping pieces.

**Browse the shelves at**
**SPEZIERIA DI SANTA MARIA DELLA SCALA**

Rome's oldest pharmacy has been closed since the 1950s, but the space, complete with its 18th-century decor, can still be toured.

**Tuck into a plate of pasta at**
**RISTORANTE PINSERIA DA MASSI**

Finish up with a warming Italian meal at this no-frills restaurant, open since the 1950s.

*On Sundays, the city's biggest flea market occupies* **Porta Portese**, *where locals and tourists alike hunt for vintage goods and antiques.*

0 metres 200
0 yards 200

Ponte Fabricio

Isola Tiberina

*Europe's oldest Jewish community first settled in Trastevere. Today, the site of an* **11th-century synagogue** *is now a slow food restaurant.*

LUNGOTEVERE RIPA

1

**Get kitted out at CIUFFETTI GIUSEPPE**

Find the perfect accessory to complete any outfit with the help of husband-and-wife duo Giuseppe and Isabella, who craft classic Italian leather goods.

LUNGOTEVERE AVENTINO

Tevere

# An afternoon shopping in Trastevere

Trastevere has long been a community of its own, away from the frenetic energy across the river. Its cobblestone streets and ivy-covered buildings hint at a love of the past, which explains why there are still plenty of proud traditional shops here. Nose around for unique artisanal ceramics, leather goods and handmade jewellery.

**1. Ciuffetti Giuseppe**
Via di Santa Cecilia 30;
06 580 3090
///hopes.bands.twisting

**2. Biscottificio Artigiano Innocenti**
Via della Luce 21;
06 580 3926
///number.chambers.bats

**3. Antica Cappelleria Mari**
Viale di Trastevere 109;
06 583 3320 6
///doors.scenes.ventures

**4. Polvere di Tempo**
Via del Moro 59, Trastevere;
www.polvereditempo.it
///rentals.nursery.blurred

**5. Spezieria di Santa Maria della Scala**
Piazza della Scala 23;
06 580 6233
///surely.monk.outpost

**6. Ristorante Pinseria Da Massi**
Via della Scala 34a, Trastevere; www.ristorantedamassi.com
///biggest.caked.oath

**11th-century synagogue**
*////kilts.slumped.arching*

**Porta Portese**
*///writings.burying.zips*

# ARTS & CULTURE

*Ancient ruins, Renaissance works, street art and churches galore: Romans proudly live alongside these icons and leave their own modern mark on the city, too.*

# Ancient Relics

***Rome definitely wasn't built in a day, as the ancient structures scattered across the city testify. For locals whizzing past temples on Vespas, these relics are precious parts of the daily scene.***

## DOMUS AUREA

**Map 4; Via della Domus Aurea, Monti; ///sprouts.gagging.asleep; www.parcocolosseo.it**

Majestic, showy, colossal: even the ruins of the "golden house" are impressive. The palace was built after the Great Fire of Rome in 64 CE, and it's where the notorious Emperor Nero preferred to host his legendary parties. More than 20 years of restoration work have made it possible to see its excavated rooms and detailed frescoes, while a VR experience lets you catch a glimpse of Roman living.

## BATHS OF DIOCLETIAN

**Map 4; Viale Enrico de Nicola 78, Termini; ///scoots.strapped.donates; www.museonazionaleromano.it**

While a bathing experience with 3,000 other people may not sound appealing, that's exactly what these 3rd-century CE thermal baths were built for. In this ancient Roman wellness space, visitors would bathe, catch up on the latest gossip and exercise. The site is unique because of its size and state of preservation: it once housed a gymnasium, a library and baths of different temperatures, a small part of which can be seen today.

## COLOSSEUM

**Map 4; Piazza del Colosseo 1, Monti; ///when.qualify.harps; www.parcocolosseo.it**

Yes, it's emblazoned across every souvenir, but the Colosseum really is the symbol of Rome (and Italians are very proud of that fact). It's a non-negotiable for most visitors, and with reason – even just a walk around the largest amphitheatre still standing reveals much about Imperial Rome and beyond.

**» Don't leave without booking a spot in advance on the Colosseum Underground tour for a fresh perspective on the site.**

Everyone and their dog has heard of the Roman Forum. But, located within a truly vast archaeological park, it's easy to find nooks and crannies for respite from the endless tourist crowds concentrated around the ruins – especially at the start and end of the day. If you're super organized, you can even grab a nice *panino* or *pizza al taglio* from one of the small shops in Monti on the way into the site for a pick-me-up snack while exploring the space.

## TRAJAN'S MARKETS

**Map 4; Via Quattro Novembre 94, Monti; ///toffee.meal.galaxies; www.mercatiditraiano.it**

Curious to see where the ancient Romans shopped? Trajan's Markets, with its multi-level structure and marble floors, looks surprisingly reminiscent of a modern shopping centre. The famous Trajan's Column is here: up close (as much as the barriers allow), you can see the intricate, sculptured images wrapped around it.

## PANTHEON

**Map 1; Piazza della Rotonda, Piazza Navona; ///rounds.removes.thankful; www.pantheonroma.com**

One of the most important buildings in Rome – and history – the Pantheon was originally built around 113 CE as a temple "for all gods" (the literal meaning of its name). Step inside for free and gawk at the sky through the round opening of the world's largest unsupported cupola, known as the Oculus. For real serenity, experience the space in the calm quiet of an early weekday morning, before the throngs of tourists arrive.

## DOMUS ROMANE

**Map 4; Foro Traiano 85, Monti; ///fall.admires.richly; www.palazzovalentini.it**

The well-to-do of Imperial Rome really were the taste-makers of their time. Form an idea of what the once luxurious interiors of their homes were like at Domus Romane. Here, beneath a 16th-century palazzo, the remains of mosaics, marble floors and wall paintings of these ancient houses hint at the grandeur that was once there. If you're finding it hard to imagine the previous finery, a new digital reconstruction helps to make sense of it.

## PYRAMID OF CAIUS CESTIUS

**Map 3; Via Raffaele Persichetti, Testaccio; ///ember.swatted.roof; 06 3996 7709**

The scene found outside Ostiense metro station hasn't changed since ancient times; you'll still find hordes of traffic, locals gesticulating passionately and – wait, is that a pyramid? Built in 12 BCE, this Egyptian-style pyramid even mystified the Romans. There's a burial chamber inside that can be seen on guided visits.

**» Don't leave without** seeing the graves of famous poets and artists who lived and died in Rome at the nearby Protestant Cemetery.

## PALAZZO ALTEMPS

**Map 1; Piazza di Sant'Apollinare 46, Piazza Navona; ///rushed.interest.lectures; www.museonazionaleromano.beniculturali.it**

If you're looking to visit just one museum in Rome, head to Palazzo Altemps, which has a show-stopping collection of ancient Greek and Roman sculpture (and some beautifully frescoed walls, too). Part of the National Roman Museum, and located right behind Piazza Navona, it used to be the private residence of cardinal Marco Sittico Altemps, after whom it's named. Its two floors are lined with a dizzying array of chiselled, white marble figures.

# City History

***Friends, Romans, countrymen: lend us your ears. Ancient times may be Rome's calling card, but they're just one part of a 2,700 year history. These places help lift the lid on its rich and varied past.***

## GALLERIA BORGHESE

**Map 5; Piazzale Scipione Borghese 5, Pinciano; ///choice.recital.exists; www.galleriaborghese.beniculturali.it**

The stories of prominent families are woven into every brick of this city. One such family was the Borghese, whose very own Scipione Borghese – a cardinal – was big on art and collected most of the works on display at this gallery bearing the family name. Paintings and sculptures are displayed across only two floors, of which the dramatic marbles by the 17th-century sculptor Bernini are the stars.

## THE JEWISH MUSEUM

**Map 1; Via Catalana, Jewish Quarter; ///miss.funny.walnuts; www.museoebraico.roma.it**

Tucked away beneath the Great Synagogue of Rome, this little museum shines a light on the long history and heritage of the city's Jewish community, dating back to the 2nd century BCE. It's located in the former ghetto, established in the 16th century and remaining in place for more than 300 years. Here, Jewish citizens were forced to lead hugely restricted lives. The small display includes historical objects and manuscripts, which tell the community's story.

## KEATS-SHELLEY MEMORIAL HOUSE

**Map 4; Piazza di Spagna 26, Campo Marzio; ///defend.bridges.bids; www.ksh.roma.it**

Literary Romanticism may not be everyone's cup of tea, but this memorial house is a celebration of creativity in the city. Based in the building where poet John Keats passed away in 1821, the collection includes the manuscripts of various British writers who lived in Rome, including Keats' pal Percy Bysshe Shelley.

**» Don't leave without** having a cream tea at nearby Babington's, a meeting place for English-speaking visitors since it opened in 1893.

## GALLERIA DORIA PAMPHILJ

**Map 4; Via del Corso 305, Trevi; ///jumpy.snake.december; www.doriapamphilj.it**

The extravagance of the Baroque is everywhere in this gallery, from the gilded halls to the art hanging within them. It's still owned by the Doria Pamphilj family (who later opened the gallery to the public); Prince Jonathan Doria Pamphilj even voices the audio tour, sharing anecdotes and ancestral stories. The most controversial painting on show is the portrait of Pope Innocent X, which shows the Pope shrewd and ageing.

## ST PETER'S BASILICA

**Map 5; Piazza San Pietro, Vatican City; ///tomorrow.sweeper.hero; www.vatican.va**

No basilica and its piazza are quite as famous as this one. Based in the independent Vatican City (located within Rome itself), it's where the Pope holds liturgies throughout the year and where many worshippers go on pilgrimage. The Renaissance architecture is a marvel – find the marble disc in the middle of the square (you'll need to battle through the crowds) to see the colonnade's rows align visually. Inside, there's a wealth of religious art to explore.

## CASTEL SANT'ANGELO

**Map 5; Lungotevere Castello 50, Vatican City; ///magazine.crab.lame; www.castelsantangelo.com**

A mausoleum, a fortress, a prison: Castel Sant'Angelo has seen it all. Once the tallest building in Rome, it was built by Emperor Hadrian in the second century, before it became a papal residence and eventually a museum over a century ago. You can learn a lot about Rome through the building alone, but the museum gives even more insight through the artworks and artifacts on show.

## SANTA MARIA DEL POPOLO

**Map 5; Piazza del Popolo, Campo Marzio; ///removal.pens.topped**

Each one of the over 900 churches in Rome – yes, 900 – is free to enter. They're the perfect stop if you're looking for places to discover art on a budget, and the 11th-century Santa Maria del Popolo has some of the best pieces. A glorious façade by Bernini, glittering mosaics by Raphael and not one but two paintings by Caravaggio are yours to explore at no cost.

## PALAZZO DELLA CIVILTÀ ITALIANA

**Map 6; Quadrato della Concordia 3, EUR; ///scope.influencing.origins**

It may take a while to get to, but this centrepiece of Mussolini's Fascist-era neighbourhood, EUR, shows a more recent side of Rome. In the quiet residential area, this palazzo eerily stands out from afar: bright white marble rises over six floors, each lined with a total of 216 identical arches. With its clean, Futurist design, the "square Colosseum" was a symbol of Fascism in Italy and remains a reminder of that past. It now draws photographers and architecture buffs, and is even home to Roman fashion house Fendi's HQ.

## VICTOR EMMANUEL II MONUMENT

**Map 4; Piazza Venezia, Monti; ///comment.rabble.luckier; www.vive.beniculturali.it/vittoriano**

Unlovingly dubbed "the wedding cake", this monument honours the first king of a unified Italy. The free museum inside tells the story of the 19th-century unification through a display of war paintings and equestrian statues. Ask a local what they think of it, and you'll hear mixed views. Whatever your opinion, its huge scale means there's a panorama at the top – and ticket holders can take the lift.

» **Don't leave without** visiting Palazzo Venezia, a Renaissance-style mansion built for Cardinal Pietro Barbo, included with the lift ticket.

# Street Art

***Beyond Rome's historic centre lies a modern open-air gallery. Graffiti artists, muralists and other creatives have chosen the city's streets as their canvas, adding a new layer to Rome's long artistic heritage.***

## BIG CITY LIFE

**Map 6; Via di Tor Marancia 63, Tor Marancia; ///remote.quicker.loud; www.bigcitylife.it**

Twenty artists from ten different nations came together in 2015 to transform this rundown neighbourhood into a bustling outdoor gallery. Using the walls of Tor Marancia's social housing as a canvas, they splashed on over 2,600 sq m (28,000 sq ft) of murals. Walk through to see everyday life and art converge: painted images across once-similar walls colour the streets as residents pass by.

## WASP'S NEST BY LUCAMALEONTE

**Map 6; Porta Furba Metro A Stop, Quadraro; ///cycled.invent.teach; www.muromuseum.blogspot.com**

Thanks to the free, open-air Museum of Urban Art of Rome, it's easy to learn more about the street art that covers the quiet Quadraro and Torpignattara outskirts. The starting point of the museum's self-guided tours (to be clear, this is no ordinary museum) is Lucamaleonte's *Nido di Vespe*, or "wasp's nest". The name and image of giant wasps across a free-standing wall allude to the area's Nazi-given nickname, a nod to its resistance to fascism.

## JUMPING WOLF BY ROA

**Map 3; Via Galvani, Testaccio; ///viewers.dressing.kneeled**

In old-school Testaccio, you'll find a 30-m (98-ft) tribute to a symbol of Rome, *la lupa*. Unlike the maternal version in museums, this beast is gnarly, sinewy and kind of angry. Painted on the side of a residential palazzo, the wolf looks pinned in by her surroundings and ready to pounce. But is anyone afraid of this big, bad wolf? No, not even the families who carry on in the playground in front of it.

» **Don't leave without** turning on your heels and heading directly into Mercato di Testaccio for an excellent street food snack.

Not many visitors make it out to the area of Quarticciolo, but those who do are rewarded with the sight of Bolognese artist Blu's 2019 addition to Rome's street art. The work features treasured Italian artworks like the Venus di Milo and David kitted out with smartphones, gold jewellery and other 21st-century trappings. The result is jarring, intentionally so, with viewers encouraged to reflect on the distracting effects of modern-day consumerism.

## Liked by the locals

**"Painting on a wall is my personal dialogue with the city: murals have meaning because of the context, colours and history that surround them. When I started painting in the late 1990s, Rome was not a city of street artists at all. Now, it has an influx of them."**

ALICE PASQUINI, STREET ARTIST

## MURALS BY BLU

**Map 3; Ex Caserma dell'Aeronautica, Via del Porto Fluviale 10, Ostiense; ///happier.obvious.fairy**

Street artist Blu spent two years creating 27 super-sized faces on the side of an old military warehouse, the building's windows becoming the eyes. Made without official authorization, the murals were produced in collaboration with the squatting residents of the building, with whom the artist stayed while working. Although some of the art has faded since original completion (in 2014), the site remains a bright and iconic feature of Ostiense.

## TRONCHI MORTI BY ANDREA GANDINI

**Map 3; Start at Giardino degli Aranci, Aventine; ///vision.haggis.mammal; www.andreagandini.art**

As authorities chopped down trees – due to disease, age and maintenance budget cuts – Andrea Gandini made the stumps left around the city his new medium, carving images into so-called Tronchi Morti sculptures. Make a morning of hunting for his works, starting with the one located in the Giardino degli Aranci.

## HUNTING POLLUTION BY IENA CRUZ

**Map 3; Via del Porto Fluviale 7, Ostiense; ///brighter.tech.boom**

Looming over one of the city's most congested crossroads is this piece by Milanese artist Federico "Iena Cruz" Massa. A blue bird with a fish in its beak, the work covers a whopping 1,000 sq m (10,700 sq ft) of walls and was created using anti-pollution paint.

# Favourite Museums

***When a city is home to one of the largest museums in the world, you know it means business. And it doesn't stop there. Rome's host of esoteric museums tell the story of its writers, food, religions and more.***

## CENTRALE MONTEMARTINI

**Map 3; Via Ostiense 106, Ostiense; ///text.dial.head; www.centralemontemartini.org**

Industrial machinery and millennia-old sculpture: it's an unexpected combination, but, somehow, it works. A power-plant-turned-gallery, Centrale Montemartini displayed Capitoline Museums artworks during renovations in the 1990s. It proved popular, so this display of ancient sculptures in front of old engines continued permanently.

## VATICAN MUSEUMS

**Map 5; Viale Vaticano, Vatican City; ///pump.elated.civil; www.museivaticani.va**

There may be endless crowds inside, but, honestly, it's worth it. The Vatican Museums hold over 70,000 works of art, accumulated by the Catholic church over the years and loved by locals and art lovers everywhere. Set aside a few hours to enjoy the immense

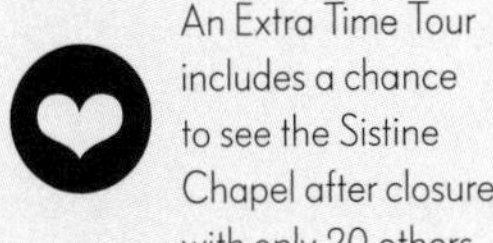


collection: the Sistine Chapel paintings by Michelangelo, Raphael's *School of Athens* and the ancient *Laocoön* sculpture are all here.

## MUSEUM AND CRYPT OF THE CAPUCHIN FRIARS

**Map 4; Via Vittorio Veneto 27, Trevi; ///edgy.radio.shoebox; 06 8880 3675**

Full disclosure: this space, known by locals as "the bone chapel", is not for the faint-hearted. Beneath the posh Via Veneto, the crypt was decorated by Capuchin friars with the remains of their brothers who were deceased. Why? As a reminder of their own mortality. An exhibition reveals more about the Capuchin's lives and beliefs, and includes objects, garments and famous artworks they collected.

## CAPITOLINE MUSEUMS

**Map 4; Piazza del Campidoglio 1, Monti; ///phones.clashes.litters; www.museicapitolini.org**

Comprising three palazzi (designed by Michelangelo, no less), the Capitoline Museums have been home to ancient Roman artifacts and Renaissance masterpieces since 1471. An unmissable piece? That'll (quite literally) be the remnants of the 4th-century statue of Constantine – its head alone is over 2 m (6 ft) tall.

» **Don't leave without** having an *aperitivo* on the Terrazza Caffarelli. The views of the Vatican across Roman rooftops are stunning.

# Solo, Pair, Crowd

**Nothing beats exploring the quirky side of history, whether it's on your own or with some culturally minded pals.**

## FLYING SOLO

### Ready player one

Gaming is the priority at Vigamus Videogame Museum. No need to bring anyone with you – you'll want to focus all your attention on trying out the game consoles from different gaming eras.

## IN A PAIR

### Better together

You'll need a friend to brave the Museum of the Souls of Purgatory. Here, there's a collection of objects supposedly marked by unfortunate souls stuck in purgatory (Italians really are obsessed with mortality).

## FOR A CROWD

### Get inventive

The Leonardo da Vinci Exhibition is best experienced with a group. It's all about immersing yourself in the genius of his inventions, so you and your mates can get hands-on with the exhibits.

## GALLERIA SPADA

**Map 1; Piazza Capo di Ferro 13, Campo de' Fiori; ///bound.remover.whizzed; www.galleriaspada.cultura.gov.it**

You're never too far from a palazzo in Rome, and this 16th-century one has a well-hidden secret. Inside its courtyard lies a forced perspective gallery: an optical illusion where the 9-m (29-ft) colonnade looks four times its actual length. Aside from this gem, the art inside the palazzo illustrates the tastes of the time.

## GARUM MUSEO DELLA CUCINA

**Map 3; Via dei Cerchi 87, Ripa; ///stocks.free.flicks; www.museodellacucina.com**

Inside this small museum you'll find Renaissance ice cream moulds, 19th-century pasta machines and early Italian recipe books on display. It's the perfect spot to stock up on niche food history tidbits to impress your friends with at your next dinner party.

» **Don't leave without** joining a guided tour where you get to taste dishes based on some of the first Italian recipes ever to be written.

## MUSEO HENDRIK CHRISTIAN ANDERSEN

**Map 5; Via Pasquale Stanislao Mancini 20, Flaminio; ///gone.welfare.veto; 06 321 9089**

The former home of Norwegian-American artist and urban planner Hendrik Christian Andersen, this quaint museum shines a light on the sculptures, busts and project drawings he left behind, many inspired by the city. Oh, and did we mention that entry is free?

# Modern Art Spaces

***Modern art and architecture often court controversy and love-it-or-hate-it opinions in Rome. Either way, there's no denying they both add a contrast to the city's famous relics.***

## GALLERIA D'ARTE MODERNA

**Map 4; Via Francesco Crispi 24, Trevi; ///breeding.hiking.slick; www.galleriaartemodernaroma.it**

Based in an 18th-century convent, this small and quiet gallery originally opened in 1883 as a city collection, holding works by well-known Italian artists like Ettore Roesler Franz and Giorgio Morandi. These days it also pays attention to documenting Rome's buzzing local art scene – its temporary exhibitions usually include works from other contemporary galleries by Roman artists.

## ARA PACIS MUSEUM

**Map 5; Lungotevere in Augusta, Campo Marzio; ///parks.easels.sounds; www.arapacis.it**

Despite its name ("Altar of Peace"), this large, sleek steel-and-glass construction by American architect Richard Meier stirs up some pretty strong feelings among Romans. Some see it as a great masterpiece, others as a gaudy petrol station. But, look beyond any debates and you'll find a typical Roman blend of old and new; the modern structure houses ancient altar fragments from 13 BCE.

## CHIOSTRO DEL BRAMANTE

**Map 1; Arco della Pace 5, Piazza Navona; ///tennis.reminds.tenses; www.chiostrodelbramante.it**

It's hard to imagine this place 500 years ago, when monks wandered its cloisters in quiet prayer. Why? Well, today Chiostro del Bramante is a women-led, buzzing cultural space all about modern art, where clued-up Romans head for bold and thought-provoking shows. The temporary exhibitions – ranging from installation works to paintings by the likes of Lucian Freud – contrast with the historical Renaissance space, visually telling a story of art history.

» **Don't leave without** enjoying an espresso in the peaceful café. There are displays of local artists' works to check out here, too.

## MUSEUM OF CONTEMPORARY ART OF ROME

**Map 6; Via Nizza 138, Salario; ///mailer.spoils.shakes; www.museomacro.it**

The Museum of Contemporary Art of Rome (MACRO to its friends) doubles as a local meeting place in well-to-do Salario. With free entry for all, creatives head here to see artworks by Italian artists from the 1960s to today. Believe it or not, this modern, glass-filled space was originally a Peroni beer production plant until the 1970s.

## GALLERIA LORCAN O'NEILL

**Map 1; Vicolo dei Catinari 3, Campo de' Fiori; ///woof.operated.method; www.lorcanoneill.com**

Looking for a contemporary art fix? Nestled into a pretty courtyard near Campo de' Fiori, this small private gallery is easy to miss. But try not to: inside are free temporary exhibitions, with previous shows including big names like Martin Creed and Kiki Smith.

## RHINOCEROS

**Map 3; Via dei Cerchi 21, Ripa; ///bland.cycle.exacted; www.rhinocerosroma.com/galleria**

Created by Alda Fendi (of the Roman fashion dynasty), this non-profit arts foundation is a culture hub, hosting a whole array of contemporary art shows in the Palazzo Rhinoceros. Love the Fendi style? Then don't miss the luxuriously decorated rooftop bar.

## FONDAZIONE PASTIFICIO CERERE

**Map 6; Via degli Ausoni 7, San Lorenzo; ///edgy.adjust.dusted; www.pastificiocerere.it**

What was once a flour and pasta factory in the city's suburbs is today a trendy art gallery in up-and-coming San Lorenzo. When the *pastificio* went out of business in the 1960s, the building owner rented out rooms to young artists who became known as the "San Lorenzo Group". These creators dismantled the machines and built walls and floors, turning the industrial space into a workable studio and exhibition space that caught the attention of art critics and enthusiasts alike. Nowadays, the building holds spaces for creative studios as well as a gallery with photography, architecture and contemporary art displays.

## GALLERIA NAZIONALE D'ARTE MODERNA E CONTEMPORANEA

**Map 5; Viale delle Belle Arti 131, Flaminio; ///jeep.items.baseline; www.lagallerianazionale.com**

A ramble around the Galleria Nazionale d'Arte Moderna e Contemporanea (GNAM) will impress anyone. Beyond the grand Neo-Classical marble entrance lie famous paintings that even the most art-adverse would recognize (we're talking pieces by Van Gogh, Mondrian and Monet, to name a few). There are also works by modern Italian artists familiar to most Romans, like Futurist painter Giacomo Balla and Surrealist artist Giorgio de Chirico.

## NATIONAL MUSEUM OF 21ST CENTURY ART

**Map 5; Via Guido Reni 4a, Flaminio; ///safari.cope.defender; www.maxxi.art**

With its concrete blocks and curves, the National Museum of 21st Century Art (or MAXXI) is the unofficial heart of Flaminio. Join the switched-on crowd for a modern exhibition or just hang in the square outside, which becomes a cultural hotspot come summer.

» **Don't leave without** hitting the gift shop, full of books and magazines on art and architecture – perfect for a curated shelf.

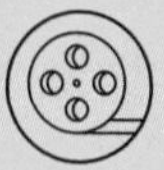

# Movie Magic

***Rome wasn't nicknamed "Hollywood on the Tiber" for nothing: the city has played countless starring roles on the silver screen. Have a magic movie moment yourself – when in Rome and all that...***

## PONTE SISTO

**Map 2; Ponte Sisto, Trastevere; ///prayers.rash.deep**

Connecting Trastevere to Rome's historic centre, the Ponte Sisto footbridge usually sees a constant stream of locals passing over it. In the James Bond film *Spectre*? Not so much. During Daniel Craig's fourth outing as 007, he jumps from a helicopter onto the bridge, miraculously free of foot traffic. (Another scene sees him chased along the Tiber in his Aston Martin by a Spectre agent.)

## CINECITTÀ STUDIOS

**Map 6; Via Tuscolana 1055, Cinecittà; ///bless.gazette.commented; www.cinecittasimostra.it**

What began as a propaganda tool under Mussolini's dictatorship developed into Europe's biggest and most important movie studios. Cinecittà has seen numerous movies filmed on its watch – *Roman Holiday, Ben-Hur, Cleopatra, The English Patient, The Passion of the*

*Christ*, *The Two Popes*, we could go on. To the delight of cinephiles, the studios were opened to the public in 2011 under the project name Cinecittà Shows Off. And it certainly does that, showing visitors its sound stages, outdoor sets and costume departments.

## FONTANA DELLE TARTARUGHE

**Map 1; Piazza Mattei, Jewish Quarter; ///fuel.cheater.leafing**

Of Rome's many, many fountains, this turtle-themed one has become a local favourite. Legend says it was built by a young, poor aristocrat in an effort to convince his father-in-law-to-be not to call off his wedding after he lost all his money to gambling. These days, it's recognized for that scene in *The Talented Mr Ripley*, where Matt Damon loads a body (we won't say whose) into the back of a car.

## VILLA DORIA PAMPHILJ

**Map 6; Via Leone XIII, Gianicolo; ///swimmer.cheese.skewed; www.villadoriapamphilj.it**

TV series *The Young Pope* wasn't actually filmed inside the buildings of the Vatican – unsurprising, we know. Instead, replicas of the Sistine Chapel, St Peter's Basilica and the Vatican Library were made and filmed at Cinecittà. As for Jude Law and Diane Keaton's long walks in the grounds of Castel Gandolfo, the Pope's summer residence, these scenes were filmed outside Villa Doria Pamphilj in Rome's largest landscaped garden *(p171)*. Spend a morning walking in their footsteps.

» **Don't leave without** catching a film at the cute indie Cinema Intrastevere, which is handily nearby.

## BATHS OF CARACALLA

**Map 3; Viale delle Terme di Caracalla 52, San Saba; ///migrate.detail.salads**

Fellini's satirical drama *La Dolce Vita* is probably most famous for its Trevi scene, when characters Marcello and Sylvia wade sensually in the fountain's waters. But the preceding scene gets to the nub of the film's message. Inside the ancient Baths of Caracalla, socialites dance wildly at a fancy supper club, their diamonds and furs flailing around them; it's this lifestyle of pleasure and excess that the movie critiques. (Admittedly a trip to the baths today is more touristy than titillating.)

## TEMPIETTO DEL BRAMANTE

**Map 2; Chiesa di San Pietro in Montorio, Trastevere; ///headache.dishes.energetic; www.sanpietroinmontorio.it**

Inspired by the works of Fellini, art house film *La Grande Bellezza (The Great Beauty)* gives an insight to life in Rome through the eyes of aging journalist Jep. In one memorable scene, Jep plays hide and seek with a young girl in a striking temple, which you'll actually find tucked away inside the Church of San Pietro in Montorio (where, it's believed, St Peter was crucified under the orders of Emperor Nero).

## BOCCA DELLA VERITÀ

**Map 3; Piazza della Bocca della Verità, Ripa; ///tilting.skipped.refuses**

Classic rom-com *Roman Holiday* includes countless shots of the city's most famous sights: the Trevi Fountain, Spanish Steps and Colosseum, to name a few. And yet one of the film's most memorable scenes is when Gregory Peck pretends to have his hand bitten off by the Mouth of Truth (or Bocca della Verità to Italians). Aside from film fans visiting to re-enact the scene, the 2,000-year-old marble mask is popular with Roman parents warning their kids not to tell lies.

## FOUNTAIN OF FOUR RIVERS

**Map 1; Piazza Navona; ///survive.bunks.dignity**

Piazza Navona is the beating heart of the city, so naturally the square has appeared in various blockbusters. Take the scene in *Eat, Pray, Love* when Liz Gilbert (played by Julia Roberts) sits on a bench alongside a couple of nuns and enjoys a gelato. Facing the bench is Bernini's Fountain of Four Rivers, where Robert Langdon saves the last cardinal from drowning in *Angels and Demons*. Oh, and then there's that scene in *The Talented Mr Ripley* where Philip Seymour Hoffman dramatically pulls up by the fountain in a cherry-red convertible.

**» Don't leave without passing by the Santa Lucia restaurant, next to the splendid Hotel Raphael. This is where Liz shows off her skills at ordering in Italian in *Eat, Pray, Love*.**

### Try it!
### MOVIE TOUR ON WHEELS

Want to live your *Roman Holiday* fantasy? Sign up for a movie-inspired Vespa tour with Scooterama (*www.scooterama.com*). The Fellini & La Dolce Vita or La Grande Bellezza tours will make you feel like a protagonist.

# A morning tour of **modern Flaminio**

Sure, Rome's ancient ruins are iconic, but there are some trail-blazing examples of modern architecture around, too. North of the centre in Flaminio, modern and old structures coexist, a reflection of the area's development. From monumental 1930s Fascist architecture to Art Deco geometry, it has a little bit of everything – including the really quite marvellous MAXXI art and architecture museum.

**1. Stadio dei Marmi**
Viale dello Stadio dei Marmi, Foro Italico
///trucked.blocking.socket

**2. Ponte della Musica**
Ponte della Musica Armando Trovajoli
///begin.uptown.suffix

**3. National Museum of 21st Century Art (MAXXI)**
Via Guido Reni 4a; www.maxxi.art
///safari.cope.defender

**4. Osteria Flaminio**
Via Flaminia 297; www.osteria-flaminio.it
///partners.jokers.cooks

**5. Vertecchi Roma - Flaminio/Parioli**
Via Pietro da Cortona 18; 06 332 2821
///tones.rental.sourced

**Little London**
*///indeed.fidget.date*

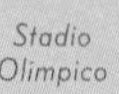


VIALE P. BOS

1

**Spot the statues at**
**STADIO DEI MARMI**
Check out this Fascist-era 1930s stadium, uniquely lined with 60 sculptures made of Carrara marble.

LUNGOTEVERE MARESCIALLO CADORNA

**Amble over th**
**PONTE DELLA MUSIC**
After a walk down th Lungotevere (the Tib waterfront), head across th Ponte della Musica. Th contemporary pedestric bridge was built in 20

VIALE ANGELICO

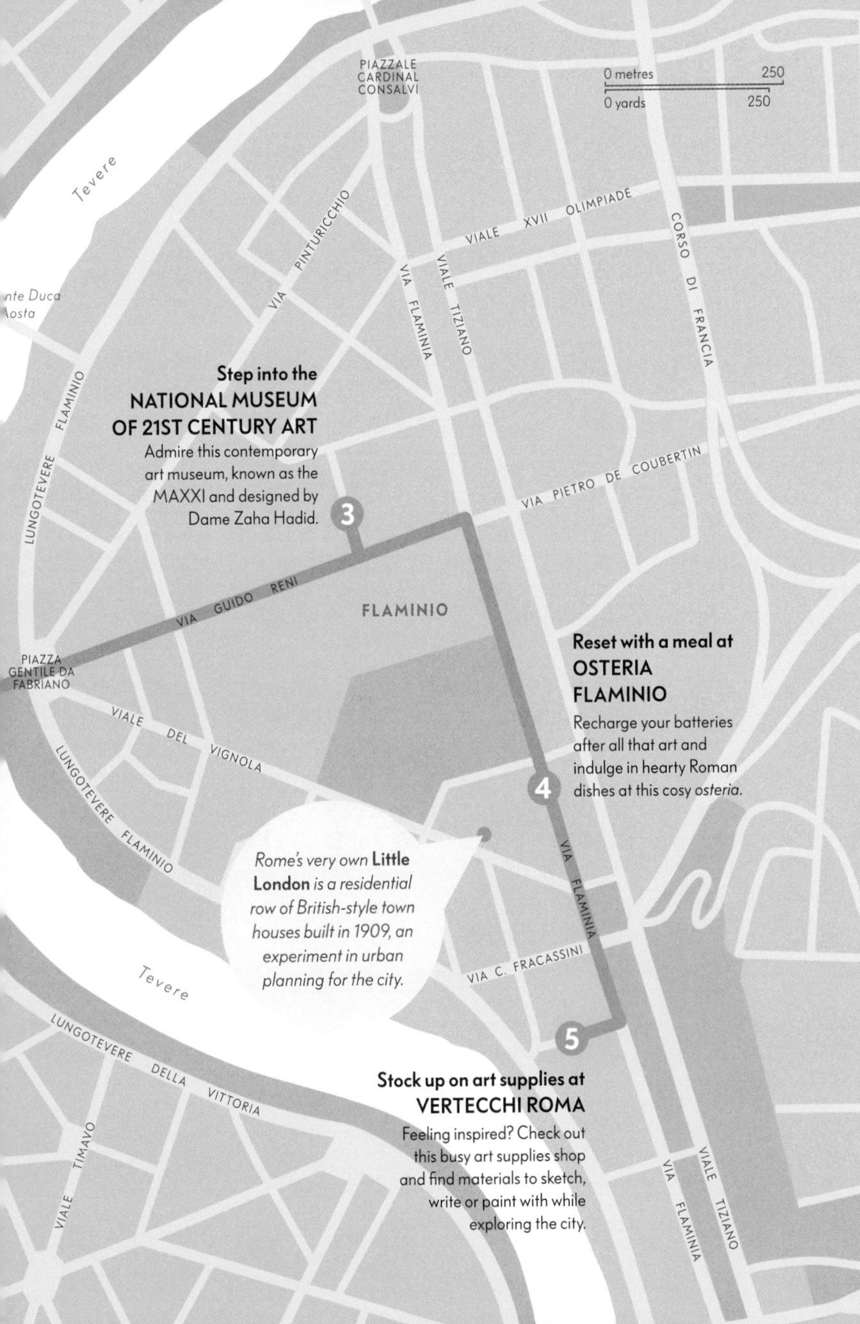
PIAZZALE CARDINAL CONSALVI
0 metres 250
0 yards 250
Tevere
VIA PINTURICCHIO
VIALE XVII OLIMPIADE
CORSO DI FRANCIA
VIA FLAMINIA
VIALE TIZIANO
LUNGOTEVERE FLAMINIO
Step into the
NATIONAL MUSEUM OF 21ST CENTURY ART
Admire this contemporary art museum, known as the MAXXI and designed by Dame Zaha Hadid.
3
VIA PIETRO DE COUBERTIN
VIA GUIDO RENI
FLAMINIO
PIAZZA GENTILE DA FABRIANO
Reset with a meal at
OSTERIA FLAMINIO
Recharge your batteries after all that art and indulge in hearty Roman dishes at this cosy *osteria*.
VIALE DEL VIGNOLA
LUNGOTEVERE FLAMINIO
4
VIA FLAMINIA
*Rome's very own* **Little London** *is a residential row of British-style town houses built in 1909, an experiment in urban planning for the city.*
VIA C. FRACASSINI
Tevere
5
LUNGOTEVERE DELLA VITTORIA
Stock up on art supplies at
VERTECCHI ROMA
Feeling inspired? Check out this busy art supplies shop and find materials to sketch, write or paint with while exploring the city.
VIALE TIMAVO
VIA FLAMINIA
VIALE TIZIANO

# NIGHTLIFE

***Just like their ancient ancestors, Romans know how to have a truly bacchanalian time. Nights begin with an obligatory* aperitivo *and end well into the early hours.***

# Aperitivo Spots

***The Italian ritual of* aperitivo *is sacred in Rome. Beginning from 6pm, it's the golden hour (or two) when locals drink, snack and say goodbye to the day before the start of the night ahead.***

## SALOTTO 42

**Map 1; Piazza di Pietra 42, Trevi; ///model.squad.workshops; www.salotto42.it**

What better way to sightsee than from a cocktail bar opposite ancient ruins, a drink in hand? Sink into one of Salotto 42's plush velvet sofas and order a martini, which will come with all the trimmings worthy of an *aperitivo* (think olives, crisps and mini canapés). There are a variety of well-leafed design books dotted around the space, too, for those after even more art inspiration.

## HEY GUEY ROOFTOP AT CHAPTER ROMA

**Map 1; Via di Santa Maria de' Calderari 47, Jewish Quarter; ///pimples.bossy.solder; www.chapter-roma.com**

Come spring, the Chapter Roma hotel throws open the doors of its rooftop bar to clued-up Romans, who know *this* is the place for unbeatable city views. There's no classic Italian wine and cured

Rooftop season is May to September. Not here then? Chapter Roma's indoor bar is open year-round.

meats here; Hey Guey is all about tacos and perfectly mixed margaritas. Take note: there's limited space out on the terrace, so be sure to book in advance.

## THE COURT

**Map 4; Via Labicana 125, Celio; ///shocking.divided.easy; www.manfredihotels.com/the-court-new**

Big anniversary on the cards? This rooftop bar of the famed Hotel Palazzo Manfredi is the perfect place to start your night. The cocktails here are beautifully crafted (with a heck of a price tag to match) but the real draw is the unbeatable view of the Colosseum illuminated under the inky night sky. Be sure to don your smartest trousers (yes, there is a dress code) and reserve ahead.

## IL MARCHESE

**Map 5; Via di Ripetta 162, Campo Marzio; ///coughed.prepare.earth; www.ilmarcheseroma.it**

This is Europe's first bar dedicated to *amaro*, an Italian liqueur traditionally enjoyed as a digestive. Here it's made the protagonist of the menu, with numerous *amaro*-infused concoctions on offer. Sip the delicacy in the bar's grand palazzo-like surroundings, inspired by the 1980s film *Il Marchese del Grillo* (which is all about a hedonistic nobleman), and mingle with Rome's upper crust.

» **Don't leave without** trying one of the bar's monthly selection of 30 *amaros* (perhaps with a splash of tonic).

## IL SORPASSO

**Map 5; Via Properzio 31/33, Prati; ///bangle.domestic.letter; www.sorpasso.info**

Every neighbourhood in Rome has an "it" bar and, in Prati, it's Il Sorpasso. Ask any local what makes it so special and you'll hear a different answer. For some, it's the bargain wine list, for others the tempting *taglieri* (platters) draped with the finest Italian and Spanish prosciuttos. Whatever the draw, it's the place friends and neighbours start the night, piling in from 6pm most evenings to catch up on the day's gossip over a glass of wine.

## DUKE'S

**Map 5; Viale Parioli 144, Parioli; ///situated.incomes.reclaim; www.dukes.it**

An *aperitivo* with a saving? Now we're talking. Take advantage of the happy hour (6–8pm) and try both the signature negroni and cosmopolitan for the price of one. The outdoor tables are perfect for enjoying a drink and some food (the Black Angus steak bites are heavenly). Just remember to dress up: it's an elegant affair.

## FRENI E FRIZIONI

**Map 2; Via del Politeama 4, Trastevere; ///keep.quieter.pizzas; www.freniefrizioni.com**

Don't expect anything fancy at this self-dubbed "street cocktail" bar. The minute the clock strikes 6pm, university students descend on this grungy spot, asking the expert barman to knock up something potent.

Things get busy quickly and it's never long before the crowd spill onto the piazza outside, leaning against lamp-posts and sitting on walls while debriefing on their days.

## TREEBAR

**Map 5; Via Flaminia 226, Flaminio; ///cooks.outlast.hills; www.treebar.it**

You don't go to Treebar for the food or drinks; you go for the vibe. Set in a pretty little garden, under the shade of Italian stone pine trees, this charming spot forms the backdrop for pals enjoying a chitchat, drink and snacks in hand. Do as the Romans do and unwind here at the end of the day, with the nonchalance typical of off-duty locals.

## BEPPE E I SUOI FORMAGGI

**Map 1; Via di Santa Maria del Pianto 9a, Jewish Quarter; ///braked.dodging.overhaul; www.beppeeisuoiformaggi.it**

Sometimes it pays to keep *aperitivo* hour classic: Italian wine, cheese, cured meats. And the setting? You want somewhere like Beppe e i suoi Formaggi, a hole-in-the wall wine shop and deli in the Jewish Quarter. Everything on the menu is carefully selected by shepherd and owner Beppe Giovale, who comes from a family of traditional cheesemakers. If you're here in summer, enjoy your *aperitivo* with a side of people-watching at one of the tables out in the alley.

» **Don't leave without** purchasing Beppe's very own cheese from the counter, surely the best possible souvenir for a foodie.

# Live Music

***Rome may be ancient, but its music culture places fresh talent centre stage. Live music really does set the scene here, whether it's laid-back jazz played in moody bars or an opera performed among ruins.***

## ROME OPERA HOUSE

**Map 4; Piazza Beniamino Gigli, Termini; ///hairpin.rankings.plug; www.operaroma.it**

For a night at the opera look no further than the glorious Rome Opera House. Nothing beats the glamour of an opening night, but, really any performance is something special. Book tickets in advance and don your finest – it's worth every penny.

» **Don't leave without** enjoying the magic of live music under the stars with a summer opera at the ancient Baths of Caracalla *(p134)*.

## AUDITORIUM PARCO DELLA MUSICA

**Map 5; Viale Pietro de Coubertin 10, Flaminio; ///blinking.sizing.outdoor; www.auditorium.com**

Of all the music venues in Rome, this one's the most epic. Aside from its huge auditorium (which seats 2,800), outdoor theatre and incredible acoustics, Parco della Musica attracts the biggest names in rock, pop and jazz, and it's also the host of the annual Roma Summer Fest. Haven't managed to bag a ticket? The impressive building designed by Italian archistar Renzo Piano is reason enough to visit.

## MONK

**Map 6; Via Giuseppe Mirri 35, Portonaccio; ///marginal.duke.means; www.monkroma.it**

On any given day, walk into Monk and you'll find anything from kids crafting in the multi-levelled garden with their parents to groups of pals chatting over drinks and street food. But the undeniable favourite among locals is the gig space inside: here, emerging local musicians regularly perform, as well as theatre groups and stand-up comedians. Head in for a show and you may discover a new star in the making.

## ALEXANDERPLATZ

**Map 5; Via Ostia 9, Prati; ///canyons.beards.possibly; www.alexanderplatzjazz.com**

Jazz fans, Alexanderplatz is for you. This world-renowned jazz bar has set the scene for laid-back nights out in town since 1984. No need to wonder if walls could talk – the ones here are covered in the graffitied scribbles by past performers, telling the story of the bar's history. Expect off-duty musicians chatting around candlelit tables most nights, praising the soft thud of a double bass during a jam session and taking in the music with a glass of wine.

# Solo, Pair, Crowd

**Whether you're on a solo tour or out with the band, there's plenty of music venues to explore in Rome.**

## FLYING SOLO

### Take to the mic

Share your musical or stand-up talents at Yellow Bar. The hostel bar regularly hosts open mic nights for a friendly crowd of travellers, and there's even an underground club where you can dance away any post-show jitters.

## IN A PAIR

### Jazz for two

On Tuesdays, the Gatsby Cafè *(p152)* goes from bistro to unpretentious jazz bar. With the band and dancing often spilling out onto the portico just outside, grab the person you're with and join in the fun.

## FOR A CROWD

### Something for everyone

Heading out-out with the gang? Bar India hosts DJs and experimental music sets from June to September – perfect for making memories with friends old and new.

## ALCAZAR LIVE

**Map 2; Via Cardinale Merry del Val 14, Trastevere; ///lunch.prude.pretty; www.alcazarlive.it**

The queue outside this former cinema is there for a reason: locals head here for guaranteed great energy. Thursdays are all about the "Come Mamma m'ha fatto" jam session, when emerging musicians play, while Fridays and Saturdays are taken over by a strong line-up of international DJs who spin soul, funk, R'n'B and disco.

## COTTON CLUB

**Map 6; Via Bellinzona 2, Trieste; ///sizzled.chuckle.brass; www.cottonclubroma.it**

The Cotton Club's weekly jazz nights are legendary, but its annual summer festival is even better. Each edition of Village Celimontana hosts jazz, swing and big band musicians from June to September in a picturesque leafy setting.

» **Don't leave without** taking part in a free swing dance class with local fans, usually scheduled before one of the shows.

## TRAMJAZZ

**Map 6; Departure from Piazza di Porta Maggiore, Esquilino; ///juices.coiling.obey; www.tramjazz.com**

If you're looking for a memorable way to experience the city's music scene, look no further. Hop aboard this working tram and glide through the centre of Rome after sunset, accompanied by live jazz and a candlelit dinner. The journey ends in the piazza at midnight.

# Hidden Bars

***Everyone loves a secret bar, hidden underground or tucked away within a restaurant, and Romans are no different. The city has a glut of speakeasies – you've just got to find your way inside.***

## THE JERRY THOMAS PROJECT

**Map 1; Vicolo Cellini 30, Campo de' Fiori; ///duke.dishing.swan; www.thejerrythomasproject.it**

If you like your cocktails classic, this spot has got you covered. Find the covert doorway on a narrow street and say the password (found on the website) to the bouncer. You'll be led into a tiny, 1920s-style bar, where leather chesterfields and live jazz performances all set a sophisticated scene. You can forget vodka, it isn't served here – one of the house rules is not to ask for it. Gin martini it is, then.

## INT. 2

**Map 5; Piazzale di Ponte Milvio 43, Ponte Milvio; ///once.blaring.lands; www.int2.it**

Well hidden on the first floor of a residential building, this intimate bar's only sign of life is the "Int. 2" label on the intercom. Once you've buzzed, head upstairs to find an apartment elegantly transformed

Many bars require a reservation and a membership card (like the ARCI card), available for €5–€10.

into a bar, complete with cosy seating and moody lighting. The friendly owners Ludovica and Federico can advise on drinks (just don't expect mocktails).

## CLUB DERRIÈRE

**Map 1; Vicolo delle Coppelle 59, Campo Marzio; ///segments.spirits.enhancement; 0329 045 2505**

Push through the wardrobe doors in Osteria delle Coppelle to find the aptly named Club Derrière. Inside this small bar, friends and couples catch up over dimly lit tables. The themed drinks menu changes yearly; in 2022, the Wonder Woman, made with gin, pomegranate, laurel and lemongrass, was the drink of the year.

## CLUB SPIRITO

**Map 6; Via Fanfulla da Lodi 53, Pigneto; ///giggles.hitters.energy; www.club-spirito.com**

Premiata Panineria restaurant is home to more than just tasty burgers. If you're just after a drink, head straight inside (the staff know the drill) and look for a secret back door labelled "Carni Scelte". One buzz of the intercom and, moments later, you'll find yourself in an American diner-turned-speakeasy, complete with red booths and a roulette wheel right on the bar. Ask one of the expert bartenders for a drink and grab some chips – poker chips, that is.

» **Don't leave without** trying your hand at blackjack on a Wednesday night – you might just be lucky enough to win a few more drinks.

## ARGOT

**Map 1; Via dei Cappellari 93, Campo de' Fiori; ///drifting.spent.tried; www.argotroma.com**

This is the more central – and secret – of this popular bar's two locations. The entrance is a barely visible corner door without a sign, through which sophisticated locals step inside. Nestled underground, couples and friends unwind in the nooks around the bar and toast to the start of the night. The rattle of ice cubes is a regular sound as slick bartenders mix drinks from the highly regarded seasonal menu. You'd be forgiven for thinking you'd landed in the roaring 1920s among all the cocktails and weekend live jazz – in other words, it's the perfect place to leisurely *carpe diem*.

## THE RACE CLUB

**Map 4; Via Labicana 52, Esquilino; ///rating.thus.emails; www.theraceclubspeakeasyroma.com**

At first glance, this spot may look like an old car repair shop (think neon signs, motorbikes and mechanical paraphernalia). But not everything is as it seems. Follow the sound of jazz and classic American tunes downstairs and stumble into a laid-back, cosy bar. Cocktails are a serious yet playful business – don't be surprised if your order arrives at your table in a baby bottle, series of test tubes or maybe with a GameBoy on the side. It's easy to drink into the early hours before re-emerging to street level, Colosseum in sight.

» **Don't leave without** ordering from the charity drink list. Part of the proceeds are donated to a cause after which the drink is named. We're particularly fond of the zesty Gin-e-tic cocktail.

## WISDOMLESS CLUB

**Map 1; Via Sora 33, Piazza Navona; ///fence.tenses.grants; www.wisdomless.it**

You might think a tattoo studio and a bar are a dangerous mix, and you're not wrong. At Wisdomless, your drinks menu arrives alongside a tattoo portfolio, so you can sip a potent cocktail while contemplating some new body art. The place feels like a swish gentlemen's lounge, with taxidermy wall mounts and a hidden drinking room. Oh, and then there's the occasional hum of a tattoo machine.

## THE BARBER SHOP

**Map 4; Via Iside 2, Esquilino; ///leafing.yappy.dishing; www.tbspeakeasy.com**

The entrance to this bar matches the name: it's all vintage barber chairs, mirrors and chequered floors. But barber shop it is not. Downstairs, bartenders mix classic cocktails, like crowd-pleasing daiquiri recipes from the 1950s. One minute you're asking for an old fashioned, the next you're heading home at sunrise.

### Try it!
### COCKTAIL WORKSHOP

Always wanted to master the art of making a negroni or an Aperol Spritz? Sign up to a Drink Italians: Cocktail Making Class at Il Marchese *(p141)* and try your hand at mixing classic Roman cocktails.

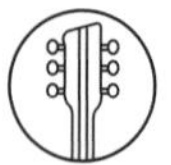

# Late-Night Entertainment

***Sure, Romans love chilling out in a piazza,* aperitivo *in hand. But, when they want to go all out, these are the revelrous venues they head to for a dose of late-night entertainment.***

## SATYRUS

**Map 5; Scalea Bruno Zevi, Flaminio; ///resting.report.ally; 327 233 2776**

Located by the gates of the dreamy Villa Borghese, this is the perfect spot to cool off after hours. The show starts before you find a table: depending on the evening, a juggler on stilts may point you to the colourful bar, or a swing band might be playing while you order a negroni *sbagliato* (with prosecco in it) under the pines.

## GATSBY CAFÈ

**Map 4; Piazza Vittorio Emanuele 106, Esquilino; ///audibly.mammal.scenes; www.gatsby.cafe**

The good folk of Esquilino are regulars at this café, popping in to read the paper, have their daily espresso and talk shop with the staff. But on Tuesday nights, things kick off like it's the Roaring Twenties.

Cappuccinos are swapped for cocktails and a jazz band keeps everyone's feet tapping into the night. Sometimes you'll even catch the band playing and Romans dancing outside the café under the portico, treating passersby to a pre-show taster. Don't be shy – join in.

## FRISSÓN

**Map 1; Via dei Cartari 7, Campo de' Fiori; ///loud.theme.unscrew; www.frissonroma.it**

You know what every town needs? A listening bar. Somewhere to enjoy a glass of wine, try out some records and chat to fellow music lovers. Frissón, created by DJ Luca and gallerist Mario, is just that. Drop by the modern space to enjoy a glass of natural wine, leaf through crates of vinyl and listen to some mellow, local tunes played by a resident DJ.

» **Don't leave without** browsing the rare vinyl and vintage books collection. We guarantee you'll find a new favourite to take home.

## LA CONVENTICOLA DEGLI ULTRAMODERNI

**Map 6; Via di Porta Labicana 32, San Lorenzo; ///dean.puff.drifter; www.ultramoderni.com**

Say ciao to Mirkaccio and Madame de Freitas: he's the showman tickling the piano keys, she's the diva crooning cabaret tunes. Together they'll show you a rip-roaring romp of a night with illusionist tricks, burlesque dances and singalongs galore. Want more? We suggest buying a membership card (it's €10 for the year, and worth every cent).

## THE MAGICK BAR

**Map 5; Lungotevere Guglielmo Oberdan 2, Prati; ///windows.siblings.marbles; www.themagickbar.com**

Come summer, Romans make their way to this riverside bar to revel in beach party vibes. Located on the Tiber, it's easy to mistake the place for a summer fiesta: drinks flow, the crowd grows and DJs keep the party going well into the night.

## STÄDLIN

**Map 3; Via Antonio Pacinotti 83, Trastevere; ///backup.harvest.trek; www.stadlin.club**

Looking for a late-night club vibe without the queues, loud music and crowds? Then this is the place to go. With great music (the Friday and Saturday DJ sets are all about contemporary techno and house music), the atmosphere is simultaneously lively, familiar and laid-back. Drinks are taken seriously at the bar, where the 40-odd gin selection takes the lead. Forget dancing, it isn't a big thing here; instead, catch-up over a G&T and check out the peaceful large outdoor space if you need a breather.

## BLACKMARKET HALL

**Map 4; Via de Ciancaleoni 31, Monti; ///surfed.zoned.export; www.blackmarkethall.com**

You and your tribe could easily spend an entire night out at this Jack-of-all-trades bar. The music, food and drinks are top tier; start with an *aperitivo* out on the leafy terrace, then head inside

If you're peckish, the kitchen is open until midnight and serves great burgers (some are vegan, too).

to the vintage-style space for cocktails with a side of bruschetta. It's easy to linger here, with a live band setting the scene well into the early hours most nights.

## HOTEL BUTTERFLY

**Map 5; Viale dei Gladiatori 68, Foro Italico; ///luring.heavy.soak; 353 409 4744**

Mime artists performing silent skits. DJs dancing to their own beats under fairy-lit gazebos. An enchanted garden. Have we stepped into another world? No, it's summertime hotspot Hotel Butterfly, an annual summer opening in the city that's always hotly anticipated. Influencers love this adult playground, posing for photos with colourful cocktails amid the venue's lush foliage.

## CASH DINER CLUB

**Map 1; Largo del Teatro Valle 4, Piazza Navona; ///join.prayers.sampling; www.cashdinerclub.it**

"Go big or go home" seems to be Cash Diner Club's unofficial motto. It's where Romans head for a dinner show with a side of razzle dazzle. Dancers, live bands and singers perform throughout the night on a small stage, covering styles from pop to rap to underground beats – all with an extravagant dash of sequins. Even the room feels theatrical, with walls covered head-to-toe in tongue-in-cheek paintings and neon lights. Don't want the night to end? Then stay for the club night, which takes over the space into the early hours.

# Cool Clubs

***Looking to go full out? Rome's got you. This is a city packed with underground clubs, grand events and LGBTQ+ hangouts. There's just one rule: don't show up before 11.30pm.***

## CIRCOLO DEGLI ILLUMINATI

**Map 3; Via di Libetta 1, Ostiense; ///braked.napkins.minute; www.circolodegliilluminati.it**

On a road that's home to Rome's underground music scene, you'll spot a lively crowd queuing to get into Circolo degli Illuminati. Friday nights are reserved for students only, but Saturday is for the masses. Each of the venue's three main rooms are dedicated to either house and techno, hip-hop or chilled beats; visit the last for a relaxed drink before enjoying a second wind on the dance floor.

## NAOS

**Map 5; Via Torrita Tiberina 6, Ponte Milvio; ///hopeless.year.change; www.naosrestaurant.com**

A stylish Greek restaurant that turns into a club may sound unusual, but trust us, it's a perfect match. On Friday and Saturday nights, the industrial-chic space (which used to be an electrical equipment warehouse) plays host to DJs. Tuck into classic Greek dishes, like aubergine meatballs and marinated lamb chops, before abandoning your table to dance into the night.

**» Don't leave without booking a table for brunch the next morning. For €35 you'll get an incredible spread plus live jazz.** ***Opa!***

## SMASH AT MOLO ZERO

**Map 5; Via Capoprati, Foro Italico; ///tend.pills.viewing; www.smashofficial.com**

Ask any student their favourite way to spend a summer Saturday and they'll inevitably say hanging out at one of the Smash club nights. Different venues host the popular event, so keep an eye on the club's website (Molo Zero is our favourite), but you can always expect the same drill: DJs amping rap, hip hop and techno beats, and everyone dancing in one big, sweaty mosh pit.

Sometimes you just want classic floor-fillers and friendly faces when you're on a night out. Thankfully, GIAM queer nights are all about crowd-pleasing hip-hop, pop and dance music, with dancers and drag queens thrown in for good measure. The inclusive party takes place every Saturday night at a different venue; keep your eye on socials to check where the next bash will take place. (GIAM stands for "gorgeous, I am" so you know you'll leave feeling on top of the world.)

## Liked by the locals

**"We can't complain about the club scene in Rome, there's so much variety. There's a definite clubbing crowd too – you will run into the same people!"**

PAOLO ARGOMENTI, CO-FOUNDER OF SOFT GELATERIA AND BONO PORK SANDWICH

## PROFUMO SPAZIO SENSORIALE

**Map 6; Via di Villa Lauchli 1, Cassia; ///scapoli.rivolti.bagnati; www.profumoroma.com**

Weekend nights at Profumo kick off with a piano bar experience, and it doesn't take long for Romans to nostalgically sing along to Italian tunes from the last century. The party carries on well into the night, when a DJ set takes over the sound systems and the dressed-up locals head to the dance floor.

» **Don't leave without** exploring the glamorous outdoor space, complete with flower-laden arches and a swing.

## MUCCASSASSINA AT QUBE

**Map 6; Via di Portonaccio 212, Tiburtino; ///curvy.ramble.region; www.muccassassina.com**

Everybody is welcome at Muccassassina, Rome's raucous and longest-running LGBTQ+ club night (it started in the 1990s). Good-timers of all communities meet on the dance floor on Friday nights to throw shapes while mixes of pop, tech and house play on.

## LANIFICIO 159

**Map 6; Via di Pietralata 159, Pietralata; ///starch.digs.caged; www.lanificio.com**

It's worth the schlep out to Pietralata for a club night at this abandoned factory. Every Friday and Saturday night, the space hosts a different event, encompassing everything from reggaeton and 1990s bangers to post-punk and queer nights.

# A night out in
# Pigneto

The severe bombing of industrial Pigneto during World War II flattened the area and led to strong anti-Fascist sentiment among its locals. It's transformed since, with a thriving creative community moving in, but that spirit of resistance remains. The people of Pigneto remain politically and culturally active, spraying murals across its walls, setting up trendy bars and food spots, and hosting popular music events. With so much variety, it's the perfect area for a great night out.

**1. Libreria Tuba**
Via del Pigneto 39a; www.librieriatuba.it
///bulges.month.avoid

**2. Sant'Alberto**
Via del Pigneto 46; www.santalbertopizzeria.com
///peanut.segments.last

**3. Necci dal 1924**
Via Fanfulla da Lodi 68; www.necci1924.com
///lighten.proceeds.airbag

**4. Fanfulla 5/A**
Via Fanfulla da Lodi 5a; www.fanfulla5a.it
///active.fresh.shrimps

**5. Co.So.**
Via Braccio da Montone 80; www.cosoroma.business.site
///aura.pointer.sweat

**Pasolini murals**
*///router.retiring.prime*



**Browse with a drink at LIBRERIA TUBA**

Start at the feminist LGBTQ+ bookshop and bar. With regular events and a "reading is sexy" philosophy, it perfectly captures the free-thinking and politically active vibe of Pigneto.

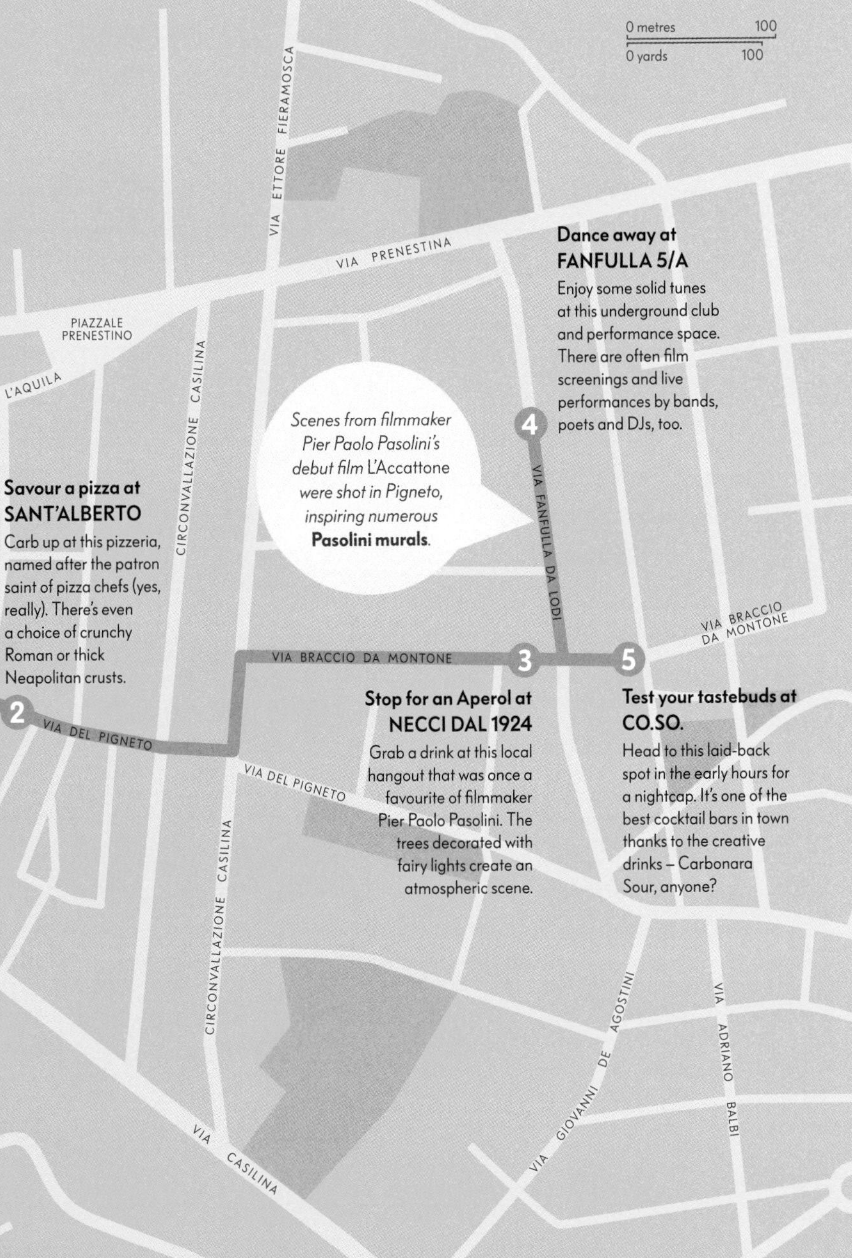
0 metres 100
0 yards 100
VIA ETTORE FIERAMOSCA
VIA PRENESTINA
PIAZZALE PRENESTINO
L'AQUILA
CIRCONVALLAZIONE CASILINA
Dance away at
FANFULLA 5/A
Enjoy some solid tunes at this underground club and performance space. There are often film screenings and live performances by bands, poets and DJs, too.
4
Scenes from filmmaker Pier Paolo Pasolini's debut film L'Accattone were shot in Pigneto, inspiring numerous Pasolini murals.
VIA FANFULLA DA LODI
Savour a pizza at
SANT'ALBERTO
Carb up at this pizzeria, named after the patron saint of pizza chefs (yes, really). There's even a choice of crunchy Roman or thick Neapolitan crusts.
VIA BRACCIO DA MONTONE
3
5
VIA BRACCIO DA MONTONE
2
VIA DEL PIGNETO
Stop for an Aperol at
NECCI DAL 1924
Grab a drink at this local hangout that was once a favourite of filmmaker Pier Paolo Pasolini. The trees decorated with fairy lights create an atmospheric scene.
Test your tastebuds at
CO.SO.
Head to this laid-back spot in the early hours for a nightcap. It's one of the best cocktail bars in town thanks to the creative drinks – Carbonara Sour, anyone?
VIA DEL PIGNETO
CIRCONVALLAZIONE CASILINA
VIA GIOVANNI DE AGOSTINI
VIA ADRIANO BALBI
VIA CASILINA

# OUTDOORS

*With so much history right on their doorstep, locals can't help but make the most of the city. Days are spent chilling in piazzas, strolling ancient roads and enjoying the view.*

# Scenic Walks

***Italians cannot bear to rush. Take the* passeggiata*: the ritual of a gentle stroll of an afternoon or evening. Walking arm-in-arm with a loved one, soaking in the city's beautiful scenery – does life get any better?***

## APPIAN WAY

**Map 6; Via Appia Antica, Appio; ///crunchy.sits.dishing; www.parcoappiaantica.it**

The queen of long-distance roads (so said poet Statius), the Appian Way is the first and most famous Roman thoroughfare. Built in ancient times, this long road stretches from Rome down to Puglia and allowed for trade and communication across the empire. Nowadays, the Appian Way is a beloved day out for cyclists, who bounce over the road's cobbles, and walkers craving some fresh air away from the city's notorious traffic. Fancy joining them? Check out our tour on p184.

## PASSEGGIATA DEL PINCIO

**Map 5; start in Piazza del Popolo, Trieste; ///soulful.dining.palms**

Passing soaring pines, decorative fountains and classical statues, this hill walk is arguably Rome's most romantic *passeggiata*. After a sumptuous Sunday lunch, loved ones saunter from Piazza del

Popolo *(p173)* and into elegant Villa Borghese *(p171)*. From there it's a bit of an incline up the Salita del Pincio path to reach the terrace at the top of the hill, but the views are completely worth it. True romantics plan their walk for late afternoon when the sun is starting to set and all of the city is bathed in that gorgeous golden hour of sunlight.

**» Don't leave without strolling via Villa Borghese's striking, self-powered water clock, which is set in the middle of an artificial lake.**

## JANICULUM HILL

**Map 2; start on Via Corsini, Trastevere; ///train.provider.rushed**

Climbing Trastevere's Janiculum Hill to hear the daily cannon fire? It has to be done at least once. Since the 19th century, a cannon has been shot on the hill every single day at noon as a way to synchronize the ringing of Rome's church bells. Satisfied for having heard the boom, continue along the hill's paths to the Fontana dell'Acqua Paola, an ornate fountain that actually inspired the spotlight-stealing Trevi Fountain.

### Try it!
### A SCAVENGER HUNT

Discover Trastevere's secret courtyards and views with a Foxtrail scavenger hunt *(www.foxtrail.it)*. Whether you're alone or with a group, you'll need a phone with data and SMS access to receive hints and clues.

# Solo, Pair, Crowd

**Looking to sketch? Planning a walk with a pal? After views with the crew? When it comes to scenic walks, Rome always delivers.**

## FLYING SOLO

### Draw on the beauty

Pine-tree-lined boulevards, mini mazes, ornate fountains: Villa Doria Pamphilj *(p133)* is the ideal spot for a solo stroll with a sketchpad.

## IN A PAIR

### Get lost in Trieste

With its village vibes, Trieste is the perfect area for a walk with a friend. There's Villa Torlonia *(p169)* and Villa Ada Savoia *(p168)* to stroll through, pretty houses to swoon over and countless coffee shops in which to re-caffeinate.

## FOR A CROWD

### Lakeside picnic with the posse

Pack a picnic and meet your friends at the train station; you're all heading to Lake Albano for the day. Gulp in fresh air and those bucolic views before an alfresco feast.

## PASSEGGIATA DEL GELSOMINO

**Map 5; start at Roma San Pietro train station, Vatican City; ///driven.bravo.flatten**

Nothing hails the start of summer like the sweet scent of jasmine, and nowhere does the perfume hang as heavily as it does in Vatican City. Top tip: the best *passeggiata* to enjoy this summertime scent is, in fact, via San Pietro train station, which sits just south of Vatican City. Head straight for platform one (you don't need to buy a ticket), walking to the very end of the platform before turning right down the Rampa Aurelia. This hidden, sloping pathway is overhung with branches of blooming jasmine. Aside from its aromatic air, the quiet little route rewards walkers with top-notch views of St Peter's dome in the distance.

## LUNGOTEVERE

**Map 1; start at Lungotevere de' Cenci, Jewish Quarter; ///bulges.jumbled.forgiven**

Few traditions start the day like an amble or jog along the Tiber, as the city unfurls from its slumber. Styled on Paris's wide, waterside boulevards, Rome's Lungotevere was built in the 19th century to stop the city from flooding (Lungotevere translates as "Tiber Waterfront"). If we're honest, you could amble along any one patch of the Lungotevere and have a sensational view, but we're particularly fond of the scenery between Tiber Island and Castel Sant'Angelo.

» **Don't leave without** walking down the steps at the crossing point of Lungotevere de' Cenci and Ponte Fabricio, which is actually Rome's oldest bridge. You'll see it up close and personal from the bottom step.

# Parks and Gardens

***Rome's parks and gardens aren't just open spaces. They're places to picnic, get away from the city and enjoy time with friends. And every Roman has a preferred spot where they go to feel closer to nature.***

## VILLA ADA SAVOIA

**Map 6; entrance via Via del Canneto, Trieste; ///bracing.mammoth.frame**

You'd never imagine an ancient, urban city like Rome would have an enormous forested park in the middle of it. With its towering stone pines and secluded trails, Villa Ada Savoia is the perfect escape on hot, dusty days. Come to relax under the shade of the park's numerous trees, dip into that holiday paperback or play a game of cards with friends.

## PARCO DEGLI ACQUEDOTTI

**Map 6; entrance via Via Appia Nuova, Appio; ///nipping.inviting.cover**

To the southeast of the city centre (not far from Ostiense), is this vast expanse of green, home to 2,000-year-old aqueducts. Sure, the park isn't as well kept as we'd like, in spite of the many lavish wedding venues that surround it. But it's hard to resist the lure of a bike ride across its pine-lined trails and around those photogenic aqueducts. Pack up a picnic and make a day of it.

## VILLA TORLONIA

**Map 6; entrance via Via Nomentana, Nomentano; ///passion.rise.sour**

Once home to the princely Torlonia family, and then Mussolini (he had a bunker here), today Villa Torlonia is an attractive hodgepodge of stately gardens and quirky buildings. Gaggles of Romans lay out picnic blankets on the park's perfectly maintained lawns and pop bottles of prosecco, the Neo-Classical Casino Nobile and fairytale-like Casina delle Civette forming a magical backdrop.

**» Don't leave without checking out the charming Serra Moresca, an Arabic-style greenhouse. Behind its façade of colourful stained glass is a collection of tropical plants and flowers.**

### Shh!

Why settle for seeing the gardens of a grand priory through a keyhole when you can get access to the key? On Friday mornings and Saturdays from mid-September to mid-June, ordinary folk have a chance to see the gardens of the Knights of Malta, who have a division here in Rome (*www.orderofmalta.int*). An expert guide will tell you all there is to know about the intimate gardens. Simply send an email to visitorscentre@orderofmalta.int to book.

## ORTO BOTANICO DI ROMA

**Map 2; entrance via Largo Cristina di Svezia, Trastevere; ///clips.chair.indicate**

Even the most no-nonsense of Romans can't resist the beauty of the Botanic Garden, which tells a different story with each season. In spring, it's the raining cherry blossom petals that lures them in; come summer, the sweet perfume of the rose garden. And autumn? The fiery colours of the Japanese Garden prove hard to resist.

## STADIO DEI MARMI

**Map 5; entrance via Viale del Foro Italico, Foro Italico; ///dialect.snoring.tangible**

We admit this stadium isn't a park in the traditional sense. Built in the 1920s as a training centre for the students of the Fascist Academy of Physical Education, Mussolini's vanity sports track sits within the city's Olympic park, Foro Italico. Intended to echo ancient arenas, the stadium is surrounded by classical-style statues holding modern sports equipment, like footballs and tennis rackets. Those who aren't unnerved by the statues' cold stares choose this space for their daily run, taking a break on the tiered stone seating when needed.

## PARCO DEL LAGO DELL'EUR

**Map 6; entrance via Viale America, EUR; ///foil.position.pizza**

Mussolini didn't stop at Foro Italico. In the south he built a business district, EUR (Esposizione Universale Roma), in celebration of the 1922 march on Rome, which was the coup d'état that enabled

Mussolini's Fascist party to seize power. With the breakout of World War II, the district didn't have the glitzy start the dictator hoped for, though its park was used in the 1960 Olympics. If you're looking for a fun spring activity, rent a boat and take in the view from the lake.

## VILLA BORGHESE

**Map 5; entrance via Porta Pinciana, Pinciana; ///secondly.season.grab**

Like the Medici of Florence, the Borghese family were a very powerful, very wealthy, noble dynasty, and this was their back garden. The grounds were landscaped in the 1600s under the instruction of Cardinal Scipione Borghese, a man who loved art and gave us the impressive collection held at the Galleria Borghese *(p116)*. In fact, the garden has the vibe of a gallery, with its artfully arranged statues, perfectly manicured lawns and charming Neo-Classical temple. It's this picturesque scenery that's inspired many a first kiss.

**» Don't leave without** visiting the French Academy, which is based in the park and hides a beautiful courtyard and 16th-century gardens.

## VILLA DORIA PAMPHILJ GARDENS

**Map 6; entrance via Via Vitellia, Gianicolo; ///breathy.reserved.carting**

On any given day, Villa Doria Pamphilj is dotted with locals enjoying an afternoon's stroll or sitting down to better savour a lunchtime panini. But Rome's biggest park really comes into its own on Pasquetta (Easter Monday): arriving at the park in their droves, families come armed with picnic rugs and baskets for extravagant all-day feasts.

# Delightful Piazzas

***Here in Italy, life revolves around the piazza. These storied settings – home to ancient monuments and ornate fountains – are used as modern-day meeting places, and everyone has their favourite.***

## PIAZZA DELLA MADONNA DEI MONTI

**Map 4; Monti; ///motivate.nodded.ponies**

Art belongs to everyone in Rome, and nowhere better embodies this than Rome's public squares, which are littered with historical artworks. Take this pretty little piazza in Monti, with its 16th-century fountain set atop a few steps. It's here, around the fountain edge, that locals sit and gossip – usually over a drink from one of the piazza's bars – just as their ancestors likely did way back when.

## PIAZZA DI SPAGNA

**Map 4; Campo Marzio; ///wage.avocado.remarked**

Sure, the Spanish Steps are a tourist hotspot but the square they sit in is lovely (it even has a tearoom). Indeed, Italian artists Giorgio de Chirico and British poet John Keats were so charmed by it that they chose to call it home. Village vibes abound, especially along ivy-clad Via Margutta, just off the piazza.

## PIAZZA DEL POPOLO

**Map 5; Campo Marzio; ///matrons.string.unites**

Vast and grandiose Piazza del Popolo was once the site of barbaric executions. Thankfully things are much more civilized these days: parents watch their kids run about the cobbles and city slickers hotfoot it through the piazza to catch the metro.

**» Don't leave without checking out the Egyptian obelisk in the centre of the square, which is estimated to be a whopping 3,000 years old.**

## PIAZZA DI TREVI

**Map 4; Trevi; ///pyramid.liners.visits**

You won't spot many locals in this piazza, not unless they're acting as tour guides for out-of-town pals. But, let's be honest, tossing a coin into the Trevi Fountain is a must (especially at sunrise when no one's about). Every year, the €1 million thrown into the fountain is donated to charity.

### Shh!

Underneath Piazza di Trevi lies a secret city – the Vicus Caprarius, or City of Water, to be precise *(www.vicuscaprarius.com)*. While construction work was underway in the piazza in the 1990s, workers discovered an underground aqueduct and apartment complex (plus coins, figurines and pottery) dating back to the 1st century. Today the ancient aqueduct, Aqua Virgo, supplies water to the Trevi Fountain above. Cool, hey? Learn all this and more on a guided tour.

## PIAZZA CAMPO DE' FIORI

**Map 1; Campo de' Fiori; ///lavender.highways.explored**

Known simply as "Campo" to locals, this piazza is always abuzz with the chatter of market traders during the week *(p85)* and the arrival of good-timers searching for a drink as dusk descends. Watching over it all, in the centre of the square, stands the angry statue of Giordano Bruno, a priest turned philosopher who was burned at the stake here for believing that the universe is infinite (no wonder he's scowling).

**» Don't leave without** visiting the adjacent Piazza Farnese, where you'll find Palazzo Farnese. The Renaissance palace houses countless artworks and hosts talks, concerts and cultural festivals.

## PIAZZA TESTACCIO

**Map 3; Testaccio; ///rare.proper.boomer**

Testaccio's *pensionati* playing the Italian card game *briscola,* kids kicking a football about, *signore* arguing over which cut of meat is superior: welcome to a typical day in Piazza Testaccio. This leafy square is, in many ways, the most Roman of piazzas. No overpriced coffees or camera-wielding tourists here; just Testaccio's famously down-to-earth community, come to unwind.

## PIAZZA NAVONA

**Map 1; Piazza Navona; ///crystal.flash.scarcely**

Why the long shape, you might ask upon arriving in Piazza Navona. Well, we'll tell you. The piazza was actually built on top of Emperor Domitian's chariot-racing stadium so its footprint mirrors its original oval shape. Of course, there aren't any nail-biting chariot races today, but there's still a sense of drama about the place. Locals weave around the square's trio of theatrical fountains, buskers and living statues perform for passing tourists, and waitstaff tout for business at the square's (pricey) pavement cafés.

## PIAZZA DELLA ROTONDA

**Map 1; Trevi; ///flashing.condiment.hardly**

Amid a tangle of streets chockful of cute stationery shops, jewellery boutiques and leather specialists sits this lively piazza. At its heart stands the iconic Pantheon *(p114)* along with a permanent crowd of passersby gazing up at the monolithic structure, awe-struck. Even Romans stop to admire the ancient temple en route to dinner at their favourite restaurants bounding the piazza, or while enjoying a leisurely evening stroll.

## PIAZZA DI SANTA MARIA

**Map 2; Trastevere; ///routine.divides.prude**

Thanks to John Cabot and the American University of Rome, you'll find more US-born students than Romans in Trastevere – well, depending on the piazza you stumble across. Piazza di Santa Maria remains a true representation of Roman life, with locals debating energetically over their espressos at the piazza's pavement cafés and *nonne* pootling about, stopping to pray in the stunning Basilica di Santa Maria. Treat yourself to a gelato and enjoy it by the fountain, taking in the scene.

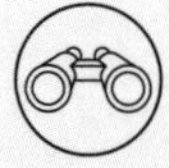

# The Seven Hills

***In ancient times, the Seven Hills of Rome signposted the city boundaries. These days the magnificent seven are more than mere markers, each with their own stories to tell – and incredible views, naturally.***

## PALATINE HILL

**Map 3; start at Via di San Gregorio, Palatine; ///goats.position.hardly**

Welcome to the most famous of the seven hills. According to legend, it was on this hill that Rome was first established by Romulus after he killed his brother Remus. Palatine went on to become a desirable neighbourhood of grand palaces and gardens, with emperors and aristocrats calling it home. That's all ancient history, of course; these days Palatine Hill is an attractive expanse of crumpling columns and weathered walls overlooking the Roman Forum *(p113)*. It's *the* place to soak up the faded grandeur of ancient Rome.

## AVENTINE HILL

**Map 3; start at Piazza Pietro d'Illiria, Aventine; ///evidently.skinny.fend**

When brothers Romulus and Remus were fighting for control, Remus chose the Aventine for his base, and we can see why – the views are top notch. Today the orange-tree lined Giardino degli

Visiting Aventine Hill in spring? Or autumn? Don't miss the Rose Garden, which has 1,100 species of rose.

Aranci, on the crest of the hill, is a popular photo spot for newlyweds, especially at sunset when the sky slips behind the horizon. *Bellissimo!*

## VIMINAL HILL

**Map 4; start at Via Nazionale, Monti; ///caked.paving.gangs**

Despite being the smallest of Rome's seven hills, Viminal is one of the busiest. Here, folks pile out of Roma Termini train station, government officials look busy as they traipse around the Ministry of the Interior and tourists make a beeline for the ancient Baths of Diocletian *(p112)*. Traffic is just as full on, especially in Piazza della Repubblica, where the hum of cars and Vespas provides a 24/7 soundtrack.

## CAPITOLINE HILL

**Map 4; start at the bottom of Cordonata Capitolina, Monti; ///slime.broker.wolf**

It's this very hill that gave us the word "capitol" (it meant "citadel" to the ancient Romans). Many say Capitoline Hill is the most beautiful of the seven, with its grand palazzi and views of the Roman Forum. And everyone agrees that the jewel in its crown is its main square, Piazza del Campidoglio, which Michelangelo designed in the 1500s. The Renaissance master knew how to impress, building a wide, scenic stairway up to the piazza, which slowly comes into view as you ascend.

» **Don't leave without** stopping for a rooftop *aperitivo* at Terrazza Caffarelli, the Capitoline Museum's lovely terrace bar.

## ESQUILINE HILL

**Map 4; start at Viale del Monte Oppio, Esquilino; ///flesh.emerge.unravel**

Once home to Emperor Nero's "Golden House", today Esquiline Hill is the most culturally diverse of the seven hills. Chinese, Thai and Ethiopian communities go about their lives here, shopping at the Mercato Esquilino *(p87)* and enjoying a pre-dinner *passeggiata* in the hilltop Parco del Colle Oppio. (This leafy park has some delightful views of the Colosseum, by the way.)

## CAELIAN HILL

**Map 3; Salita di San Gregorio, Celio; ///revival.shades.recovery**

Caelian often gets the cold shoulder in favour of its neighbour, the illustrious Capitoline. But it shouldn't: this hill hides away countless historic treasures, including truly stunning churches, like the mosaicked Basilica of San Clemente, and ancient Roman houses.

» **Don't leave without** strolling through Villa Celimontana, a delightful garden dotted with fountains by Italian sculptor Bernini.

## QUIRINAL HILL

**Map 4; start at Via del Quirinale, Trevi; ///presses.wing.when**

The President of the Italian Republic lives atop this, the tallest of the Seven Hills. And, lucky for you, the president is happy for visitors to see inside his home, the Quirinal Palace, for a very affordable €1.50. After visiting, stay a while to admire the cityscape from Piazza del Quirinale's terrace. You can't beat the Roman skyline.

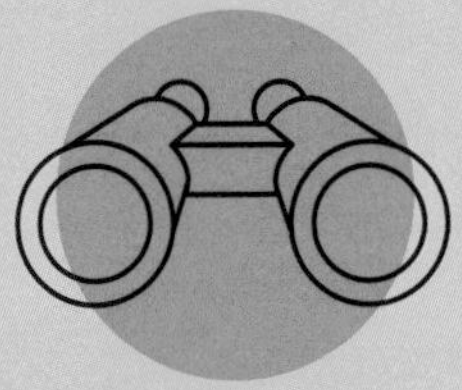

## Liked by the locals

**"As the sun sets, Rome's colours become more vibrant, and the city's sights look more incredible than ever. It's not about taking pictures – any sunset is about living in the moment."**

ARNALDO LUCA LATINI
BOARD MEMBER OF EUROPEAN ENGINEERING

# Nearby Getaways

***It's hard to part with Rome, but sometimes locals need a break from the city. Luckily, the Lazio region is home to charming hill towns, perfectly manicured gardens and truly tranquil lakes.***

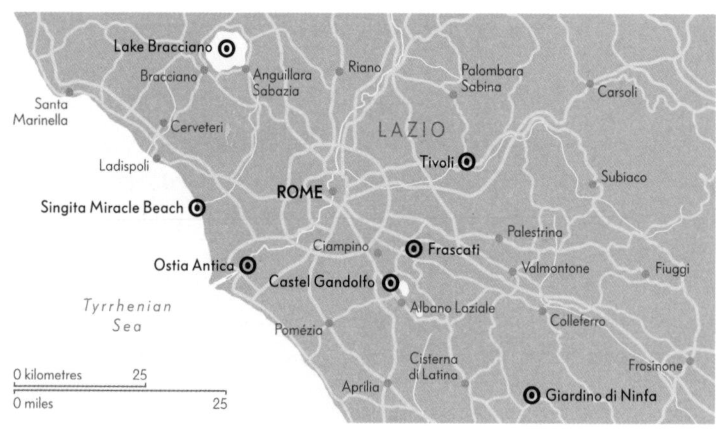


## TIVOLI

**40-minute train from Roma Termini station; www.visittivoli.eu**

Romans hate to hear it, but the town of Tivoli is said to be even older than the Eternal City (it was founded by a Greek from ancient Thebes). Historical rivalry aside, locals agree that the hillside town is utterly charming, with its archaic villas, pretty grottoes and tumbling waterfalls. Emperor Hadrian was certainly fond of it, building a fabulous retreat here before Cardinal Ippolito II d'Este plundered the villa to decorate his own Renaissance palazzo, in the 16th century. A weekend stroll around either of these fabled homes and their gorgeous gardens is welcome respite from the hubbub of Rome.

## SINGITA MIRACLE BEACH

**1-hour drive from Rome; www.singita.it**

For locals, summer holidays mean one thing: long, lazy days lounging on Singita Miracle Beach. Groups of friends pile into their cars, armed with sunnies and swimmers, driving in convoys to this sandy beach on the Fregene coastline. Here they rent four-poster sunbeds from the beach club, tearing themselves away for a quick paddle in the sea before returning to their loungers to sip mojitos at sunset.

## FRASCATI

**1-hour drive from Rome; www.visitcastelliromani.it**

When the weekend rolls around, Romans are called to the sleepy Castelli Romani (or "Roman castles"), a clutch of idyllic little towns set in Lazio's vine-draped hills. Frascati is the local favourite thanks to its crisp white wine of the same name. Enjoy a glass in one of the town's wine cellars, perhaps after a stroll around the beautiful gardens of Aldobrandini or the town's striking cathedral. And it would be rude not to sample some locally reared porchetta while you're here.

» **Don't leave without** eating at Fraschetta, a rustic osteria typical of the Castelli Romani. It's just the spot for a charcuterie board.

## OSTIA ANTICA

**15-minute train from Roma Tiburtina station; www.ostiaantica.beniculturali.it**

Forget Pompeii; Ostia Antica is just as rich in its archaeological finds and feels like even more of an adventure. Sure, the ancient harbour city isn't as big or dramatic as Pompeii but, unlike its rival, the site doesn't have ruins cordoned off. You'll get a real feel for life in the seaport as you explore its warrens of thermal baths, grand theatres, frescoed bars and mosaicked piazzas. If you're lucky, you might even catch an opera performance in the amphitheatre.

## GIARDINO DI NINFA

**1.5-hour drive from Rome; www.giardinodininfa.eu**

Sun-baked ruins adorned with wisteria, meadows dotted with colourful wildflowers and buzzing bees, blossom trees reflected in the crystal-clear water of a mini lake. Welcome to Ninfa, a fairy-tale-like garden planted around the remains of a medieval village. This is the day trip Romans roll out when they're planning a romantic rendezvous. Not that they can be spontaneous: the garden is open sporadically from March to November, and tickets must be booked in advance.

## CASTEL GANDOLFO

**1-hour train from Roma Termini; www.visitcastelliromani.it**

Back in the 17th century, Pope Urban VIII decided he needed a summer abode, somewhere he could relax and keep cool. He settled upon Castel Gandolfo, a pretty town in the Castelli Romani with gorgeous views over Lake Albano. The residence passed from pope to pope, each putting his stamp on the place. During World War II, Pope Pius XII opened the palace doors to Jewish refugees; later, Pope John Paul II had a controversial swimming pool added to the grounds. Today, the grand Apostolic Palace and its landscaped gardens are open to the public, and best enjoyed before an *aperitivo* in one of Castel Gandolfo's elegant restaurants.

## LAKE BRACCIANO

**1-hour train from Valle Aurelia station**

We know, Rome can be pretty uncomfortable in summer. And that's why suffering locals escape to Lake Bracciano, just north of the city, on their days off. Some pack up picnics for a scenic lakeside lunch, others stop for a bite in the lovely medieval town of Bracciano itself. And some make it an excuse for a weekend away, continuing on to villages like Anguillara Sabazia or Mazzano Romano for an overnight stay. Whatever the itinerary, nothing is as welcome as a plunge in the lake's icy, emerald-blue waters.

**Try it!**

### COUNTRYSIDE COOKING

Learn from the masters by booking onto a cooking workshop in Mazzano Romano (*www.theinternationalkitchen.com*). You'll pick your ingredients from a kitchen garden before whipping up something delicious.

1

**Set off from**

**CENTRO SERVIZI APPIA ANTICA**

Rent a bike and get ready to explore – just book in advance to guarantee your ride.

2

**Check out the**

**CATACOMBS OF SAINT SEBASTIAN**

Join one of the 45-minute tours to see the underground tombs and frescoes dating back to the 2nd century CE.

3

**Make a pit stop at the**

**MAUSOLEO DI CECILIA METELLA**

Visit one of the best-preserved ancient burial sites, commissioned by a wealthy Roman consul.

4

**Refuel with a**

**PICNIC**

Make sure to pack a picnic; the Roman ruins along the way are the perfect spot for a *panini* and Campari soda.

5

**Slow down and see the**

**TOMB OF HILARUS FUSCUS**

Walk your bike and see the row of tombs that begins with the Tomb of Hilarus Fuscus.

6

**Admire the luxury at**

**VILLA DEI QUINTILI**

Take in the incredible ruins of one of the Roman Empire's most opulent villas. It once belonged to the Quintili brothers, two wealthy consuls who were killed under Emperor Commodus.

*At the 1960 Rome Olympics, Ethiopia's Abebe Bikila ran barefoot along the ancient* **Appian Way** *in the men's marathon.*

VIA APPIA NUOVA

QUADRARO

VIA TUSCOLANA

VIA APPIA ANTICA

TOR MARANCIA

VIA ARDEATINA

VIA DI GROTTA PERFETTA

VIA ERMINIO SPALLA

VIA DI VIGNA MURATA

VIA APPIA ANTICA

0 kilometres 1

0 miles 1

# An afternoon cycling **the Appian Way**

It's not every day that you find yourself on one of the oldest roads in the world. Connecting Rome to Brindisi, the Appian Way is lined with tombs, monuments and around 300 km (186 miles) of catacombs. Romans today love to cruise down by bike, taking in the lush surrounding nature courtesy of the Appian Way Regional Park. Not a cyclist? Never fear: it's a flat, cobblestone road on the whole, but keep an eye out for a handful of bumpy sections and the crossroads.

*Detour to the ancient aqueducts at* **Parco degli Acquedotti**. *Word to the wise: the route here involves some busier roads.*

**1. Centro Servizi Appia Antica**
Via Appia Antica 58–60;
www.ecobikeroma.it
///podcast.planet.portable

**2. Catacombs of Saint Sebastian**
Via Appia Antica 136;
www.catacombe.org
///theme.baked.havens

**3. Mausoleo di Cecilia Metella**
Via Appia Antica 161
///hurray.spotty.scoring

**4. Picnic**
Via Appia Antica
///snails.ledge.chilled

**5. Tomb of Hilarus Fuscus**
Via Appia Antica
///slurred.solves.decks

**6. Villa dei Quintili**
Via Appia Antica 251;
www.parcoarcheologico appiaantica.it
///salsa.tiger.incurs

***With a little research and preparation, this city will feel like a home away from home. Check out these websites to ensure a healthy, safe stay in Rome.***

# Rome

## DIRECTORY

### SAFE SPACES

Rome is a friendly city but, should you feel uneasy or crave community, there are spaces catering to different sexualities, demographics and religions.

**www.arcigayroma.it**
*A community centre offering support and events for the LGBTQ+ community.*

**www.differenzadonna.org**
*A database of women's associations offering support and legal advice for victims of violence.*

**www.romaebraica.it**
*A Jewish community centre that also lists kosher restaurants on its website.*

**www.unobravo.com**
*Online therapy centre offering mental health services for English-speakers.*

### HEALTH

Healthcare in Italy isn't free to all, so make sure you have comprehensive insurance; emergency healthcare is covered by the European Health Insurance Card (EHIC) for EU residents and the UK Global Health Insurance Card (GHIC) for those from the UK. If you do need medical assistance, there are many pharmacies and hospitals.

**www.farmaciediturno.org**
*A directory of the city's pharmacies and emergency services.*

**www.medinaction.com**
*Private clinic connecting you with English-speaking doctors 24/7.*

**www.paideiahospital.it**
*A private hospital offering high-quality, personalized medical care in Rome.*

**www.regione.lazio.it**
*Official portal for healthcare in Lazio, with information on local clinics.*

**www.salvatormundi.com**
*A private hospital that cares for both local and international patients.*

**www.salute.gov.it**
*Italy's Ministry of Health, offering general advice and information on the nearest hospitals and clinics.*

## TRAVEL SAFETY INFORMATION

Before you travel – and while you're here – always keep tabs on Italy's latest regulations and security measures.

**www.esteri.it**
*The official website of the Italian Ministry of Foreign Affairs, featuring up-to-date safety and regulation information.*

**www.poliziadistato.it**
*The civil branch of the police force, with information on staying safe, emergency service numbers and reporting crimes.*

**www.protezionecivile.gov.it**
*The Italian Civil Protection website, providing information on disaster management and emergency response.*

**www.visitlazio.com**
*Lazio's official tourism website, listing useful telephone numbers and safety advice.*

## ACCESSIBILITY

Rome is gradually improving when it comes to accessibility but nonetheless its cobbled streets prove tricky for those with reduced mobility. Here are some useful websites and resources.

**www.atac.roma.it**
*Rome's official public transport website, offering information and advice on the accessibility of the metro and buses.*

**www.disabili.com**
*Tips and resources about accessible travel in Italy, including a list of accessible museums and sites in Rome.*

**www.rfi.it**
*The Italian railway infrastructure, Rete Ferroviaria Italiana (RFI), with information on getting help at railway stations, including Roma Termini station.*

**www.turismoroma.it/en/roma-accessibile**
*Rome's official website for visitors with disabilities, detailing the city's accessible attractions, transport and accommodation options.*

# INDEX

# ACKNOWLEDGMENTS

**Meet the illustrator**

*Award-winning British illustrator David Doran is based in a studio by the sea in Falmouth, Cornwall. When not drawing and designing, David tries to make the most of the beautiful area in which he's based; sea-swimming all year round, running the coastal paths and generally spending as much time outside as possible.*

**Main Contributors** Liza Karsemeijer, Emma Law, Federica Rustico, Andrea Strafile
**Senior Editor** Lucy Richards
**Senior Designer** Stuti Tiwari Bhatia
**Project Editor** Tijana Todorinovic
**Designer** Jordan Lambley
**Proofreader** Stephanie Smith
**Indexer** Helen Peters
**Senior Cartographic Editor** Casper Morris
**Cartography Manager** Suresh Kumar
**Cartographer** Ashif
**Jacket Designers** Jordan Lambley, Sarah Snelling
**Jacket Illustrator** David Doran
**Senior Production Editor** Jason Little
**Senior Production Controller** Samantha Cross
**Managing Editor** Hollie Teague
**Managing Art Editor** Sarah Snelling
**Art Director** Maxine Pedliham
**Publishing Director** Georgina Dee

MIX
Paper | Supporting responsible forestry
FSC™ C018179

This book was made with Forest Stewardship Council™ certified paper – one small step in DK's commitment to a sustainable future.
**For more information go to www.dk.com/our-green-pledge**

## A NOTE FROM DK EYEWITNESS

The world is fast-changing and it's keeping us folk at DK Eyewitness on our toes. We've worked hard to ensure that this edition of Rome Like a Local is up-to-date and reflects today's favourite places but we know that standards shift, venues close and new ones pop up in their place. So, if you notice something has closed, we've got something wrong or left something out, we want to hear about it. Please drop us a line at travelguides@dk.com

First edition 2023

Published in Great Britain by Dorling Kindersley Limited, DK, One Embassy Gardens, 8 Viaduct Gardens, London SW11 7BW, UK

The authorised representative in the EEA is Dorling Kindersley Verlag GmbH. Arnulfstr. 124, 80636 Munich, Germany

Published in the United States by DK Publishing, 1745 Broadway, 20th Floor, New York, NY 10019, USA


23 24 25 26 10 9 8 7 6 5 4 3 2 1



A CIP catalog record for this book is available from the British Library.

A catalog record for this book is available from the Library of Congress.

ISSN: 1542 1554
ISBN: 9780 2416 3305 2

Printed and bound in China.

www.dk.com